The
CHELSEA
B O O K
past and present

First published 2003
by Historical Publications Ltd
32 Ellington Street, London N7 8PL
(Tel: 020 7607 1628)

ISBN 0 948667 89 3
British Library Cataloguing-in-Publication Data
A catalogue record for this book is available from the British Library

Typeset by Historical Publications Ltd
Reproduction by Square Group, London SE1
Printed in Zaragoza, Spain by Edelvives

The Illustrations

Illustrations are reproduced by kind permission of the following:
The Cadogan Estate: *19*
Chelsea Football Club: *35*
Chelsea Harbour Estate Management: *36*
Roger Cline: *1, 15, 17, 25, 28, 33, 34, 43, 52, 61, 81, 85, 105, 111, 118,
127, 140, 146, 147, 151, 167, 181*
Royal Borough of Kensington & Chelsea: *16, 38, 39, 48, 64, 75, 87, 119,
121, 122, 133, 138, 145, 150, 161, 174*
David Le Lay: *63*
National Portrait Gallery: *77, 86*
All other illustrations were supplied by Historical Publications

The
CHELSEA
BOOK
past and present

John Richardson

HISTORICAL PUBLICATIONS

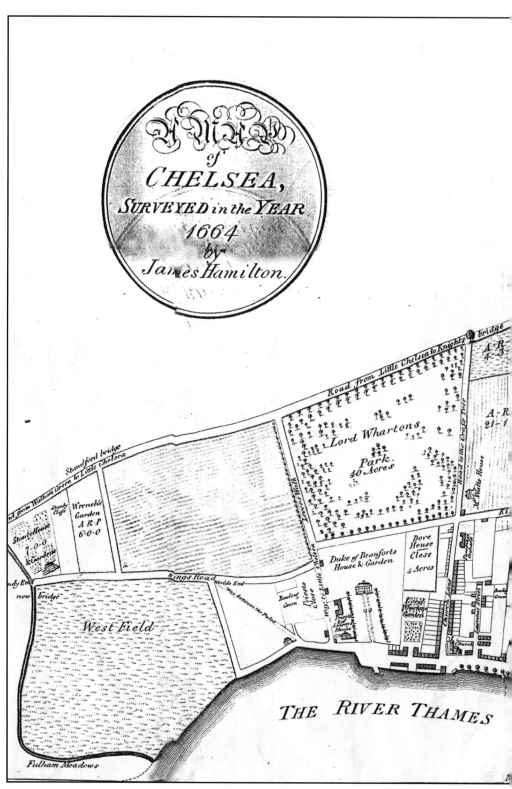

James Hamilton's map of the parish of Chelsea, 1664, as amended c.1685.

Part of Kensington Parish

Knightsbridge

Spring Gardens

A·R·P
11-1-12

A·R·P
11-1-5

Wiltshires Ground & Barns

M.ʳ Calloways formerly call.ᵈ a Flounders field & Quail Close

Heath Close
A·R·P
4·0·0

A·R·P
7·0·6

A·R·P
10·0·0

A·R·P
6·2·3

A·R·P
15·0·0

A·R·P
5·2·5

Pond and Pits

Lady Mathews House

Chelsea Common
A·R·P
37·0·7

Lord Cheynes Lands
A·R·P
8·0·24

A·R·P
7·3·23

A·R·P
4·3·2

Black Lands House

·P
5

A·R·P
4·3·24

A·R·P
6·1·3

Part of East Field

Kings Private Road

Robins Garden

Glebe
A·R·P
6·3·28

East Field
A·R·P
29·2·28

Acres

Acres

M.ᶜ Franklins Houses

Close
·R·P
3·5

Ship House & Gardens

College Court

Fleets Garden

Stone bridge

Burial Ground

Governors Garden

Gardens
·20

M.ᶜ Watts Garden

Paradise Row

Light House

Earl of Ranelaghs House & Gardens

W.ᵐ Clemens House

Stable Yard

Drying Yard

Apothecarys Garden
A·R·P
3·2·0

Earl of Orfords
1·2·0

Kitchen Garden

Introduction

Very few people can resist the charms of Chelsea. This is partly the problem, for Chelsea has become vastly expensive for house-buyers and has lost that slightly shabby but gregarious nature that once was so enjoyable and welcoming. It is now in thrall to a retailing boom in which clothes, antiques, bars and restaurants predominate. These have all but squeezed out what old Chelsea residents would regard as useful shops, although Peter Jones makes up for many of the losses.

This may be a phase that doesn't last, for the history of London has taught us above all that very little in the way of fashion or retailing, stays the same. Whatever happens it seems unlikely that Chelsea, away from the King's Road, will lose its many charms. There are difficult hurdles for any would-be developer, and in Chelsea there is a particularly vigilant Chelsea Society that aims to 'protect and foster the amenities' which are the very reason that visitors come. This is not to say that the area is mothballed. Large developments have taken place, or are imminent, in the centre and on the edges. The Duke of York Square on the site of the old Royal Military Asylum has transformed one end of the King's Road. To the south-west the defunct Lots Road Power Station awaits an expensive redevelopment – Chelsea Harbour (actually just over the border in Fulham) has shown that a formerly derelict area can be made acceptable. Changes will inevitably occur in Manresa Road when the Chelsea Art College moves out to Millbank, and in Sydney Street when the Brompton Hospital moves to Paddington.

This book is intended to highlight much of the history of events in Chelsea, from its Tudor heyday by the river, to its legendary artistic era during the twentieth century, to the modern developments. It also seeks to reveal some of the many charms of the area, usually unseen by the tourist or the shopper, and quite often not sought out by residents either.

I am grateful to Richard Tames for kindly reading the first draft of the text and making a number of helpful suggestions.

John Richardson

The Adam and Eve

The picturesque Adam and Eve pub lay by the river, west of the Old Church – it is seen below in one of Walter Greaves's evocative drawings of a commercial Chelsea riverside in the 1870s. Its galleries overlooked the river and stairs ran down to the water. The building was probably 17th-century, and its walls were festooned with fowling pieces, a reminder of the time when this marshy area by the river was popular with those anxious to kill birds.

Joseph Addison

Addison (1672-1719), strictly speaking, was a Fulham resident since he lived at Sands End, a large house on Chelsea Creek, but on the Fulham side of it. He was, however, a familiar figure in Chelsea, especially as his collaborator in so many things, Richard Steele, lived in Cheyne Walk and the pair had many meetings in Don Saltero's coffee house (qv) nearby. Addison, a confirmed Whig, was also a friend of Jonathan Swift, who in 1711 spent some months in Old Church Street. Perhaps Swift

2. Joseph Addison

had been attracted to the area having dined with Addison at Sands End in 1710. It was, in any case, an unlikely friendship as Addison was a major influence in the Whig paper, *The Tatler*, founded by Steele in 1709, and Swift had founded the Tory journal, *The Examiner* in 1710.

The Tatler, which appeared three times a week, ceased publication in January 1711, for reasons which are still unclear. But Steele and Addison replaced it with the much more successful *The Spectator*, in March the same year.

During Addison's Chelsea Creek days he pursued an extended courtship with the widowed Lady Warwick of Holland House. Addison was an old family friend and took an interest in the education of her son. He and Lady Warwick were married in 1716, whereupon Addison moved to the social whirl of Holland House. But it was not a happy relationship, possibly due to the disparity in their social and financial positions. Dr Johnson commented that the match 'resembled the marriage in which a sultan gives his daughter a man to be her slave', and there are reports that Addison used to escape Holland House for the modest surroundings of coffee houses when he could.

The Albert Bridge

The Albert Bridge is one of the more spectacular of Thames crossings and appears in stark contrast to the rather heavy and mundane architecture of the Embankment. Opened for passenger traffic on 31 December 1872 and fully opened on 23 August 1873, it helped to promote the development of middle-class Battersea in the area west of Battersea Park.

The opening ceremony for this remarkable structure, oddly, was not memorable. *The Times* reported that:

'On this occasion, perhaps 100 people were assembled about noon at a wooden barrier placed across the Chelsea end, and guarded by two policemen. An omnibus and two or three cabs were drawn up in front of the Pier Hotel, which had dressed its first-floor windows in honour of the occasion... but no other signs of an approaching ceremony were visible in the neighbourhood. Shortly after 1 o'clock the police-

1. The Adam and Eve pub on the Chelsea riverside. A drawing by Walter Greaves before the Embankment was built.

3. The Albert Bridge, soon after it opened.

men removed the barrier, and the bridge was open – that is to say, any one might, on payment of the customary Toll, for the work is a private speculation, - walk, ride, or drive across at his or her pleasure.'

The bridge, as with other London bridges, was later bought by the Metropolitan Board of Works and freed from tolls.

This hybrid of a suspension bridge was designed by R M Ordish (who had also done the much-admired roof of St Pancras station) utilising the same system he had devised for a bridge over the river in Prague. It was a popular feature of the landscape, though frail when traffic became much heavier. In the 1950s the London County Council wanted to demolish it as being inadequate, but a campaign was waged, led by John Betjeman, which saved it. Betjeman declared that 'shining with electric lights, grey and airy against the London sky, it is one of the beauties of the London river'.

Argyll House

A group of early and largeish houses, nos. 211-217, still survive in the King's Road, of which Argyll House at 211 is the most notable. This was built in 1723 for John Perrin by the Venetian architect Giacomo Leoni, but obtained its name from the residence of the 4th Duke of Argyll in 1769-70; Perrin's initials are still in monogram form in the wrought-iron gate. Leoni himself describes it as 'A little country house…upon the King's Road between Chelsea and London … the Kitchen, Buttery and other offices are within the Basement. The apartments are of a size, suitable to a private Family. The door in Front is Doric, with two columns and two half Pilasters…'

The house's best-known resident was Lady Sybil Colefax (1874-1950), who entertained in a lavish style here, rivalling and usually excelling the hospitality of Syrie Maugham next door. The comparison of the notoriety of the guests, rather than the

4. Sybil Colefax

standard of entertaining, was no doubt the subject of below-stairs gossip.

The house was transformed when the Colefaxes took up residence in 1922. Sybil had a keen eye for decorative effects, and supervised the colour schemes throughout, trying as much as possible to push the house back

5. Argyll House at 211 King's Road.

6. Dr Thomas Arne.

to its Georgian style. Wood panels were stripped of paint, Victorian fireplaces taken out, and beautiful furniture, especially lacquer, introduced. It was a much admired interior.

Most of the notable names of the era (she left in 1937) sat in her comfy armchairs – Arnold Bennett, Virginia Woolf, Hilaire Belloc, Beerbohm, Churchill and Yehudi Menuhin – were just some. According to an article by Kirsty McLeod in the *Chelsea Society Annual Report* (1997), Fred and Adele Astaire entertained the guests one evening, and on one occasion George Gershwin played the piano with Artur Rubinstein and Cole Porter standing on either side of him. The evening was rounded off by a rendering of folk songs by Jan Masaryk, son of the future Czech President. Sybil 'collected all the intellectuals around her as a parrot picks up beads', complained Virginia Woolf. Colefax joined John Fowler in establishing the well-known interior design firm of Colefax & Fowler. No plaque to Sybil yet adorns no. 211, but there is one for film director Carol Reed at no. 213.

Dr Arne

Thomas Arne (1710-78), the composer, settled for his last years at 215 King's Road. Arne, son of an upholsterer in Covent Garden, had to hide his musical ambitions when young because his father intended him for a legal career. Arne's talent in both musicianship and composing, however, convinced his father not to stand in his way, and gradually he achieved a firm reputation. Not much of his music is played today, but his reputation is assured for his composition of the patriotic song *Rule Britannia*. This was first played at a masque in a makeshift theatre at Cliveden in 1740 before an audience which included the Prince of Wales. In 1745 he was engaged as composer to the pleasure ground of Vauxhall Gardens and he also composed music to be played at Ranelagh Gardens in Chelsea *(qv)*.

Charles Robert Ashbee

Ashbee (1863-1942) was a leading arts-and-crafts designer, silversmith, specialist in church restoration and architect, whose most enduring achievement was the foundation of the London Survey Committee, a prosaic name for a body which has contributed enormously to our knowledge of the history of London. Ashbee was instrumental in forming the influential Guild of Handicrafts in 1888.

His principal Chelsea connections have, alas, been lost. When the Magpie and Stump *(qv)* public house in Cheyne Walk was destroyed by fire in 1886, Ashbee designed three houses

7. *Charles Robert Ashbee*

(nos. 37, 38 and 39) on the site, one of which, no 37, he called Magpie and Stump. This was a home for his mother as from 1894 but he established his own architectural office there as well, on the site of the old skittle ground. This house, alas, was demolished in 1968 despite a public enquiry and replaced by apartments entirely out of scale for that part of Cheyne Walk. Ashbee had his own house, which he designed, at 74 Cheyne Walk. He left here in 1902 when he moved the Guild to Chipping Campden. The next occupant of no. 74 was the painter, Whistler (*qv*), who remained here until his death. The artist, who didn't like the house, described it as a 'successful example of the disastrous effect of art upon the middle classes.' Sadly, this house was lost to a landmine in 1941.

Mary Astell

About a hundred years before Mary Wollstonecraft published her celebrated *Vindication of the Rights of Women* (1792), a Chelsea woman issued a similar declaration of independence for women. In 1694 was published her *Serious Proposal to Ladies for the Advancement of their True and Greatest Interest*, a book which questioned the nature of marriage. A woman could, she remarked, be 'yoked for life' in an arranged loveless marriage and 'denied her most innocent desires for no other cause but the will and pleasure of an absolute lord and master whose follies a woman cannot hide and whose commands she cannot but despise at the same time as she obeys them.'

She urged women to spend more time in acquiring knowledge rather than spending hours at the looking-glass. 'Your Glass will not do you half so much service as a serious reflection on your own minds .... 'Twill not be nearly so advantageous to consult with your Dancing-Master, as with your own Thoughts....'

Astell recognised that it would be difficult for many women to do this, and proposed the establishment of a secular 'convent' in which 'pious and prudent women', pledged to celibacy and scholarship, could live a contemplative life. This enraged a number of Church dignitaries, who thought it smacked of Popery. Those who opposed her included Chelsea neighbours, Steele and Addison (*qv*), and also Dr Francis Atterbury (*qv*), who said that he generally avoided discussions with her, that he found her a little offensive and shocking in her expressions, but still of an extraordinary nature, considering they came from a woman.

Mary Astell (1668-1731), well-educated by her clergyman uncle in Newcastle, came to London when she was twenty and soon settled in Chelsea at a house in Swan Walk opposite the Physic Garden. She died here and was buried at Chelsea Old Church.

Astell is commemorated on a plaque which was unveiled on the east wall of More's Chapel in the Old Church on 27 October 1934. This recorded the local residence of four distinguished women. Apart from Astell, the plaque included Margaret Roper, the daughter of Sir Thomas More, the artist Elizabeth Blackwell (*qv*) and Lady Danvers, the mother of the poet George Herbert. The plaque, by sculptor Mary Gillick, was funded by the British Federation of University Women at Crosby Hall and the Chelsea Society.

Dr Francis Atterbury

Atterbury (1662-1732) was a turbulent priest in the heady days of the Hanoverian succession to the Crown. Well-versed in ecclesiastical history and law, he was a popular writer on religious matters and took holy orders in 1687. He was a considerable preacher and, to the chagrin of other better qualified hopefuls, was appointed lecturer at St Bride's in Fleet Street, and later became chaplain to William and Mary. He was popular with Queen Anne, but increasingly found himself on the side of the Jacobites, in favour of the return of the Stuart line to the throne in the form of James III. In this he had a great deal of support, but after he had established direct links with the Jacobites abroad in 1717, he was increasingly at odds with the authorities. In 1722 Atterbury was imprisoned in the Tower for seven months and then stripped of all his church offices by the House of Commons, though he had the support of many of the London clergy. In 1723, unrepentant, he was obliged to go into exile in France and died there.

For many years, from 1685, he lived in Old Church Street, Chelsea, where he was a friend of Jonathan Swift and, despite their political differences, of Joseph Addison (qv).

8. Dr Francis Atterbury

Jane Austen

The celebrated author was not a Chelsea resident, but sometimes stayed here at the houses of her brother Henry, a Covent Garden banker. She was at his house at 64 Sloane Street in March 1811, when correcting proofs of the first of her books to be published, *Sense and Sensibility*, which had been written as long before as 1797 and rejected by publishers. It was only when Henry and his wife put up the money for its publication that it was taken on by a cautious publisher called Egerton. That book was not her first – *Pride and Prejudice* had been written in 1796, and only because of the success of *Sense and Sensibility* did it reach publication in 1813.

In a letter home to her sister, Cassandra, Jane describes a musical evening at the house in Sloane Street. The orchestra arrived in two hackney cabs, and there were sixty guests in the reception rooms.

In 1813, Henry, by then a widower, moved to 23 Hans Place, off Sloane Street, where Jane visited him several times. Her reputation was then established and in that year she received an invitation to meet the Prince Regent at Carlton House and was invited to dedicate her next book, *Emma*, to him. A specially

9. Jane Austen.

11. Battersea Bridge, looking towards Battersea, c.1838.

bound copy of the work was sent to him, but it is not known if the Prince ever read more than a few pages.

Battersea Bridge

In 1766, when an Act of Parliament was passed to build Battersea Bridge, there were no bridges across the Thames between Westminster and Putney. Travellers going south-west often went down to Chelsea and then across on the Ferry (qv) to continue their journey. The Act was promoted by Earl Spencer, who owned manorial land on the other side of the river in Battersea (and the Ferry itself), and it was in his interest to encourage travel to the south bank so as to foster development there. The bridge was open for pedestrians in 1771, and for carriage traffic the following year.

It was a picturesque structure, beloved of Chelsea's artists, in particular Whistler and Turner, but it was a serious hazard to boats because of its nineteen narrow spans, which required careful navigation. Furthermore, it was built in wood by Henry Holland, and needed constant maintenance and strengthening. However, it was the first wooden bridge across the Thames to be lit, by oil lamps in 1799 and by gas in 1824.

When the Albert Bridge (qv) was built in 1873 its proprietors were obliged to buy Battersea Bridge and to bring it up to a better standard. This necessitated some concrete strengthening. In 1879 the Metropolitan Board of Works took it over. By then it was unsafe and it was restricted to foot passengers only in 1883 and taken down altogether four years later. Its loss was bemoaned by Chelsea residents, and its replacement is a stolid, uninspiring piece of work by Joseph Bazalgette, completed in 1890.

10. Battersea Bridge from the Chelsea side, before the building of the Embankment in the 1870s. In the distance is the bridge of the West London Railway.

12. A toll house on Battersea Bridge, 1830. From a watercolour by E Hassell.

13. Twilight at old Battersea Bridge. Oil painting by James A McNeill Whistler 1876/77.

Beaufort House

Sir Thomas More's old house by the Thames was the most important mansion in Chelsea until its demolition in the 18th century. After More and is family *(qv)* the house was occupied by a number of aristocratic owners, including Sir Robert Cecil, who had possession in 1597. In 1627 it was granted by the king to George Villiers, 1st Duke of Buckingham and on his death his family continued to live there until the State seized it during the Civil War. In 1682 it came into the hands of Henry, Marquess of Worcester, the later Duke of Beaufort. It was during Beaufort's time that the well-known Kip/Knyff view, *(ill. 14)*, was made. It was as well the view was produced, for in 1737 the new lord of Chelsea manor, Sir Hans Sloane *(qv)*, demolished the house, and its site and its grounds were added to those of Sloane's manor house.

The house lay astride today's Beaufort Street, towards the King's Road.

Beaufort Street

As noted above, the street was laid out across the site of Beaufort House and its grounds, as from 1766. Illustrious residents have included the artist Roger Fry (1866-1934), at no. 29 from 1892-6, and the novelist Elizabeth Gaskell (1810-65) (born at 93 Cheyne Walk), who was at no. 7 from 1827-29. The ill-fated soldier General Gordon (1833-85) lived in the street before his expedition to Khartoum, from which he did not return. The

The House att Chelsey in the County of Middlesex one of the Seats
Marquesse & Earle of Worcester Baron Herbert of Chepstow Raglan & Gower

14. The Knyff/Kip view of Beaufort House in 1699. This is Sir Thomas More's old house – from the steps down to the river, More took his last journey to Lambeth. To the right are the gardens of Danvers House.

of the Most Noble & Potent Prince Henry Duke of Beaufort
and Knight of the Most Noble order of the Garter.

I.Kyp.

13

poet Thomas Sturge Moore (1870-1944), was at at no. 31 in 1895 where he befriended the artist Charles de Sousy Ricketts (1866-1931) who was at no. 51 until 1902.

John Bignell

John Bignell (1907-97), followed in the steps of Chelsea's principal photographer James Hedderley (*qv*). Both used their cameras at crucial times in the history of Chelsea – Hedderley just before the Embankment altered Chelsea's relationship with the river, and Bignell before the exploitation of Chelsea became very commercial indeed. Bignell did not settle in Chelsea until soon after the last war, and his work therefore encapsulates the barrenness of the 1940s, and the upturn of the ensuing two decades. To quote from his obituary in the *Chelsea Society Report* of 1998, he captured 'the empty streets and children playing cricket on sundappled roads; painters drinking Algerian wine in ramshackle studios; the final, tacky days of the Chelsea Palace music-hall; students' bed-sitter-land; Chelsea Pensioners in the pubs; and latterly, miniskirts and punks in the King's Road.'

Bignell, a tall man, was well known in Chelsea. He lived at the Manse, overlooking the Moravian burial ground at the corner of King's Road and Milman's Street.

The Black Lion

The Black Lion at the corner of Paultons Street and Old Church Street is now called The Front Page. The earlier building, shown here, was probably 17th-century, and was rebuilt towards the end of the 19th century. The Chelsea historian, Alfred Beaver, complained that 'to compare this quaint old structure with its

15. *The Black Lion in Old Church Street, probably c.1880. Photograph by James Hedderley.*

successor is to see at a glance what we are losing in this vast city of ours by the gradual purposeless destruction of all that is delightful to the eye.'

Elizabeth Blackwell

Elizabeth Blackwell (1688-1758) appears on the plaque dedicated to distinguished Chelsea women affixed to the More Chapel in 1934 (*see Mary Astell above*). She too lived in Swan Walk, from 1734, a few years after the writer's death. Blackwell is known for her 500-odd depictions of the plants in the Physic Garden, which she engraved and coloured herself, with the encouragement of the Keeper of the Garden and of Sir Hans Sloane. These were published in 1737 as *The Curious Herbal*. Her husband, Alexander, whom she had supported financially by her labours, went off to Sweden where, mysteriously, he was arrested for treason and tortured before being executed. Elizabeth survived him by eleven years and was buried in Chelsea churchyard.

The Blue Bird Company

No. 350 King's Road is now Conran's popular Bluebird Café and Restaurant, but the building itself is redolent of the 1920s when it was a very upmarket garage of a kind quite unknown to London at the time. The *Morning Advertiser* noted that 'it will provide London with one of the finest garages in the world. In this three-floored building, the upper two storeys will be suspended from the roof, so that the ground floor will be free of supporting pillars.' A steel turntable will be positioned at each entrance 'so that no matter how crowded the floor space … cars may be easily backed into a small corner'.

The *Financial Times* remarked that 15 cars could obtain petrol at the same time (for it was also a filling station), and it would also contain repair shops and car showrooms, together with lounges and club rooms for customers. To celebrate their first anniversary, the *Daily Sketch* announced, the Blue Bird Company was reducing the cost of petrol from 1/5d per gallon to 1/4d.

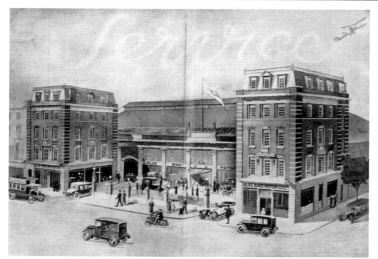

16. The Blue Bird garage in King's Road, as depicted in an advertisement in the 1920s

Reginald Blunt

Chelsea owes a great deal to Reginald Blunt, born in 1857 and brought up in the Chelsea Rectory where his father was Rector. He could remember being taken to see the formidable Thomas Carlyle, and could recall Chelsea without an Embankment, when it was much more of a riverside town.

Distressed by the rapid physical changes that were occurring in Chelsea in the 1920s, Blunt formed the Chelsea Society (*qv*) to protect its architecture and nature and was for many years the Society's secretary and moving spirit.

He had the good fortune to have a flat in Carlyle Mansions with a view of the sweep of the river, but he must have been devastated in 1941 when a landmine destroyed his beloved Old Church and much of the property near him. He died in 1944 before there was even a hope that the church could be rebuilt.

He wrote a splendid poem in the style of the *Walrus and the Carpenter*, in which he described the rapacity of local developers.

17. Reginald Blunt.

Some of it is as follows:

> The Builder and the Architect
> Were walking close at hand
> They wept like anything to see
> Such old, old houses stand.
> 'If those were only cleared away'
> They said, 'it would be grand'....
>
> 'The time has come,' the Builder said,
> 'To talk of chromium baths,
> Of service lifts and swimming pools,
> And crazy pavement paths,
> Of radio sets in every room
> And smart electric hearths.'

Brompton Hospital

This renowned hospital, now fully titled the Royal Brompton and National Heart Hospital, began life in a single building in Smith Street, Chelsea.

It was founded by a solicitor, Philip Rose, who was distressed that a clerk in his office could not get hospital treatment for his tuberculosis because the disease was so infectious. Rose's new, but small, hospital was opened in 1842.

Things moved quickly, for in 1844 the Prince Consort laid the foundation stone for the mock Tudor building on the Kensington side of Fulham Road, designed by F J Francis which, in recent years, has been turned into apartments.

When the National Health Service was established in 1948 the Brompton became the centre of expertise for dealing with chest diseases.

In 1982 the hospital moved to a large new building in Sydney Street, back in Chelsea, but it is planned to move once more, this time to the Paddington Basin.

The Bun House at Chelsea

The famed Chelsea Bun House was just east of the Chelsea border by the river Westbourne in what is now Bloomfield Terrace – Bun House Place nearby is a reminder of the enterprise. To its east lay open fields all the way to Grosvenor Place, and the area was regarded as a good day out by the river. The Bun House began in the early 18th century, and was run by four generations of the Hand family. The premises consisted of a single-storey building with a colonnaded front, which protected the many who queued outside. It was claimed that on Good Friday 1829 a quarter of a million buns

18. *The Chelsea Bun House in the eighteenth century.*

were sold – no doubt an exaggeration, but an indication of the shop's popularity. It was often visited by members of the royal family including George II, his queen and the princesses, and by Queen Charlotte, consort of George III.

An early description of the bun says that it was a 'zephyr in paste, fragrant as honey and sweeter in taste... flaky and white as if baked by the light... soft and doughy and slight...'

The building was demolished *c.*1840 when Belgravia was developed.

19. *The 5th Earl Cadogan.*

The Cadogan family

The form of much of Chelsea, not to mention many of its street names, reflect developments put in hand by the Cadogan family which owned the manor of Chelsea from the later 18th century – it made up about half of Chelsea parish. The Cadogan name first appears locally upon the death of the lord of the manor, Sir Hans Sloane, in 1753, at the age of 92. His property was then divided between his two daughters, Sarah (who had married George Stanley of Paultons in Hampshire) and Elizabeth, the wife of Baron Cadogan of Oakley. Eventually the ownership of about three quarters of the manor – then 270 acres – was held by the Cadogan family, while the balance was retained by Sloane's great nephew, also Hans, a holding which later became the Sloane-Stanley estate in west Chelsea.

A number of the finest streets in Chelsea were developed by the Cadogan Estate or their agents. In the 19th century the 5th Earl (1840-1915), the first mayor of Chelsea, made a significant contribution to Chelsea's fabric, for it was during his time as head of the Estate that Cadogan Square and the redevelopment of the Hans Town area occurred.

In 1902 the Estate sold a 20-acre site, comprising the greater part of the old Chelsea Common (*qv*). Very soon after that the remodelling of Sloane Square went on apace with the construction of the large building on the south side of Sloane Square,

20. No. 52 Cadogan Square, a highly decorated exterior.

cal base for the Royal Philharmonic Society. The premises are also to be available at times for public use, either to listen to concerts or to visit exhibitions there.

Cadogan Square

The Square is on the site of Henry Holland's grand house and grounds *(see Hans Town)* and was built in the late 1870s and 1880s by the Cadogan and Hans Place Estate Ltd. It was one of the first significant developments in London using red brick, instead of the usual yellow brick and stucco.

Nos. 62, 68 and 72 are by R. Norman Shaw, and the house in the north-east corner, in Gothic style, was designed by G E Street, the architect of the Law Courts in the Strand.

Illustrious residents have included: John Hay Beith, soldier and writer (1876-1952), at no. 21 in the 1930s; Arnold Bennett (1867-1931) at no. 75, 1922-30, in which time he wrote *Riceyman's Steps* and *Imperial Palace*; the writer Radclyffe Hall (1880-1943) *(qv)*, at no. 59 from 1911-15; Ian Hay, playwright (1876-1952) at no. 21; Moira Lister, the South African actress (born 1923), at no. 31 by 1972, having previously been at 52 Hans Place; the writer Dennis Wheatley (1897-1977) at no. 60 from 1960-70.

Mrs Patrick Campbell

Beatrice Stella Campbell (1865-1940), always known as 'Mrs Patrick', after the man she eloped with and married in 1884, first went on the stage in 1888. But the turning point in her career was in 1893, when George Alexander, later to be a resident of Pont Street, gambled on her still untried talent, and

21. Mrs Patrick Campbell, the best-known actress of her time.

chose Campbell to take the lead in a new and controversial play by Pinero called *The Second Mrs Tanqueray*. She was an outstanding success and her career hardly faltered until the next century. Though continuing to act, she also went into theatre management, taking on the Prince of Wales theatre in the West End, though this was never financially successful. Her last highly-praised role was her Eliza Doolittle in an early production of *Pygmalion*. Though devoted to her husband (who was killed in the Boer War in 1900), she kept up an intimate correspondence with George Bernard Shaw.

Mrs Campbell lived at 15 Tedworth Square and in the last twelve years of her life at 64 Pont Street.

Thomas and Jane Carlyle

A great deal has been written about the Carlyles and their residence at 24 Cheyne Row – the house is now open to the public. Thomas (1795-1881) was a literary giant of his era, re-

designed by Amos Faulkner for the developer William Willett (1856-1915), whose main claim to fame was to persuade the government to adopt the annual system of changing the clocks by one hour to save daylight time.

When the 7th Earl Cadogan succeeded to the title in 1933 he inherited 100 acres of Chelsea and substantial death duties. He had the choice of selling Chelsea to pay these and concentrate his resources on the grand family home of Culford, or vice versa. He wisely chose to keep Chelsea and the Cadogans have continued to have a substantial influence in modern Chelsea matters. The 7th Earl, who died in 1997, was the last mayor of Chelsea.

There have been many occasions since the formation of the Chelsea Society in 1927 on which the Estate and the Society have disagreed – especially about the Cadogan proposals for a massive development north of Sloane Square in 1962. However, it is fair to note that in 2000 the Estate repurchased the former First Church of Christ, Scientist in Sloane Terrace, and plans to convert the building into a musi-

23. *Jane Carlyle; portrait by Samuel Laurence.*

22. *Thomas Carlyle in his sound-proofed attic study.*

nowned for what became a classic book on the history of the French Revolution, and many other works. On previous short-lived visits to London, the impecunious Carlyle had lodged at houses in a far less salubrious area of London, near King's Cross, but in 1834 Leigh Hunt found him and his wife Jane this house in Cheyne Row, in which he stayed until his death – Jane died in 1866.

The Carlyles took up residence on 10 June 1834, arriving in a hansom cab with a canary, to be welcomed by Leigh Hunt and his wife. The rent was £35 per annum. In truth the thrifty and orderly Jane Carlyle was rather disapproving of Mrs Hunt, who seemed not to have any regard for housekeeping which was described by Hunt himself as 'hugger-mugger, unthrifty and sordid'. Mrs Hunt, who bore seven disorderly children, later took to drink.

Carlyle described the area: '…we are a genteel neighbourhood; two old ladies on one side, unknown character on the other, but with 'pianos'. The street is flag-pathed, sunk storied, iron railed, all old-fashioned and tightly done up; looks out on a rank of sturdy old pollarded lime-trees standing there like giants in tawtie wigs…'

Jane's many letters reveal details of local life, such as her dealings with Carless the butcher, Shakespeare's Dairy and Allsop the chemist. She was a very capable woman who subdued her own ambitions to look after Carlyle.

Carlyle worried about street noise, to the extent that he had an attic room sound-proofed. He was particularly irritated by cocks crowing in adjacent gardens. If he had done the housework, which of course he did not, he would have been concerned too that there was only one tap in the house, and that was in the kitchen, for which he paid £1 16s 0d per annum. Extra water supply was obtained from street pumps.

Carlyle wrote most of his important works here, including *The French Revolution* (1837). He had to rewrite much of this epic study, for he lent the only manuscript of the first volume to John Stuart Mill for him to assess but, to the dismay of everyone concerned, Mill's maid thought it was scrap paper and used it to light a fire. Five months' intensive work went up in flames.

In his later life Carlyle was much criticised. He was against increasing the electoral franchise, was enthusiastic for the militarism of the Prussians and was generally anti-Liberal, yet he was host at Cheyne Row to many forward thinkers such as Dickens, Thackeray, Darwin, Mill and Robert Owen.

Carlyle had the rare distinction, in 1872, of having a street, or in this case a square, named after him while he was still alive, when Oakley Square became Carlyle Square. His house in Cheyne Row was bought by a group of admirers in 1895 and eventually presented to the National Trust.

Joseph Boehm's statue of Carlyle in Cheyne Walk gardens, was unveiled in October 1882 at a ceremony which Robert Browning attended *(see ill. 75).*

24. The Chelsea Arts Club in Old Church Street. The Club moved here in 1902.

CHELSEA ARTS BALL
1949

25. Programme for the Chelsea Arts Ball in 1949. Ted Heath and Oscar Rabin played that evening.

Chelsea Arts Club

The Chelsea Arts Club, comfortably and gregariously ensconced at 143 Old Church Street, was founded in 1891 by a group of artists led by sculptor Thomas Lee. Founder members included Whistler, Sickert, George Clausen, Frank Brangwyn and Steer, who originally met at the home of the Scots painter, James Christie, at 181 King's Road. In 1902 the Club moved to the present premises, which have a splendid garden graced by a fountain sculpted by Henry Pool. Members have included John Singer Sargent and Henry Tonks and the scientist, Alexander Fleming. Good meals are served in an ambience of interesting paintings on the wall donated by past and present members.

In 1908 the Club instigated the renowned Chelsea Arts Ball, a grand fancy-dress party held on New Year's Eve. It became a very large affair. For example, in 1949 the music was provided by Ted Heath and Oscar Rabin and their bands, together with the Dagenham Girl Pipers who, no doubt, piped in the new year.

There were verbal and musical contributions from London art colleges; more music followed and the closing time was 5 am.

However, the event became progressively riotous at Chelsea Town Hall and then at the Royal Albert Hall, providing annual copy for newspapers in the very week in the year when it is difficult to find news. The Ball was prohibited in 1959, though it was revived in 1984.

Chelsea Barracks

Since boundary changes in 1899 the Barracks have been in Westminster, but were originally within Chelsea. The first buildings, designed by George Moore, were opened in 1862 for 1,000 foot guards. The present barracks were built 1960-66, designed by Tripe and Wakeham.

Chelsea Bridge

The line of Chelsea Bridge is believed to be that of a ford across the Thames when, in earlier times, the river was much wider and shallower. The 18th-century historian William Maitland noted that the Thames at times here was only about 4 feet 7 inches deep.

In July 1948 – well after the building of the Embankment had made the river deeper – a Mr Joe Simms, aged 51, claimed to have walked across the river at this point, with his head above water, in 17 minutes. There seems to have been some doubt as to whether he actually had his feet on the ground during this event.

26. Married quarters at the Chelsea Barracks in the 1920s.

27. *The first Chelsea Bridge.*

The first Chelsea Bridge, a suspension bridge, was built by the government and designed by Thomas Page. It opened in March 1858 and despite the fact that public money had been used to construct it, a toll was exacted for its use until its cost had been surpassed by the revenue. Unfortunately, because it needed constant strengthening, it never did recoup its outlay and it was not freed of tolls until the Metropolitan Board of Works took it over in 1879. Though the *Illustrated London News* had welcomed its design – 'a fair structure, with its beautiful towers gilded and painted to resemble light coloured bronze and crowned with large globular lamps diffusing sunny light all around' – there was no opposition from the Chelsea Society when it was demolished in the mid 1930s. The present, rather bland structure, designed by G Topham Forrest and E P Wheeler, was declared opened by the Prime Minister of Canada in May 1937.

Chelsea, Brompton and Belgravia Dispensary

The institution of free dispensaries during the earlier part of the 19th century was intended to provide medical care, even hospitalisation, for people too poor to afford a doctor's fee. Dispensaries were funded by more affluent local residents who then had the privilege of nominating patients for treatment.

The Chelsea Dispensary was founded in 1812 in Sloane Square by the Rev. George Clark, with the support of such luminaries as William Wilberforce. It began with an average of 1,200 patients a year, but by the 1880s this had increased to nearly 7,000.

Chelsea College

'King James's College at Chelsea', founded by Dr Matthew Sutcliffe, Dean of Exeter, was incorporated in May 1610 'to this intent that learned men might there have maintenance to aunswere all the adversaries of religion' – in other words, a college for clerics. This 'controversial college', as it was often referred to, was formed at a controversial time, with the new king struggling to enforce some kind of conformity in religious beliefs and practice in the vacuum left by Queen Elizabeth's death in 1603.

The project, to be built on land now part of the Royal Hos-

28. The proposed Chelsea College.

pital Chelsea, pleased neither the High Anglicans nor the Puritans, and certainly not the Catholics. Neither did it get the funding it was promised and very little of it was built, probably only the central portion which, in 1652 was described as a four-storeyed brick structure, 130 feet in length by 33 feet in depth. It comprised an entrance hall, two parlours, a kitchen, six large rooms and four closets on both the first and second floors, and a long gallery on the top floor. Parts of its foundations exist below the Royal Hospital Infirmary.

No more than four of the proposed seventeen Fellows were ever in residence, and during the Civil War the Royalist Rector of Chelsea claimed possession as Provost. In effect the project failed in this period, for in 1651 the building was taken over by the State and used as a prison, mainly for foreign captives.

The College was on Crown land and at the Restoration it reverted to the ownership of Charles II who promised that it should be used by the newly-formed Royal Society. This didn't happen, for again war intervened and the building was once again used as prison for Dutch and Swedes in 1665, the year of the Great Plague. There were many deaths amongst the inmates. During excavations in West Road in 1838, 'two human skeletons and a great quantity of human bones' were discovered, and in 1907 further remains were found.

The College building deteriorated more: the tiles were taken off and timber was stored to prevent further decay. In the end its site was sold to enable the building of the Royal Hospital which, confusingly, in its early days was known as a 'College'.

The site is shown on the map on pp 4-5. This plan, originally surveyed in 1664 and updated in 1717, shows the beginnings of the Royal Hospital on the site of the Chelsea College.

Chelsea Common

What used to be Chelsea Common is bounded today by Fulham Road, Sydney Street, Cale Street, Elystan Place and Draycott Avenue. Hamilton's map of 1664 *(pp 4-5)* shows the parish Poor House on its western extremity, a pond and gravel pits on its north west (Pond Place today is a reminder), and

29. Chelsea Common in 1769.

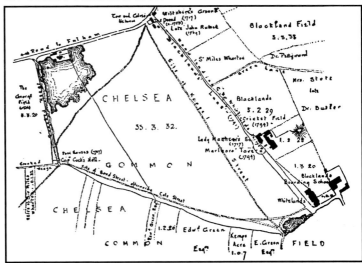

a total extent of about 37 acres. The Common was, in theory, owned by the lord of the manor, but some local residents had rights of common – to graze their animals, to gather wood etc, fiercely defended by law. In 1790 the Cadogans obtained an Act of Parliament enabling them to enclose the land and a development of low-grade houses was the result, described by one Chelsea historian as 'a labyrinth of streets, mainly narrow and squalid'.

In modern times a resident of these streets, A C Tearle, saw the area rather differently. It was, as recorded in the *Chelsea Society Annual Report* (2001), a friendly district, self-contained, self-sufficient, with useful local shops. Reminiscing in 1964 about the 1890s, he was able to remember the shops with remarkable clarity, in an era of horses, of children playing in the streets and a life of very few luxuries indeed.

One tradesman, a German called Linke, ran a coffee shop and as a sideline kept chickens in his front yard by the pavement. The local chimney sweep each May Day instigated his own weird procession of a tower covered with leaves. Tearle recalled that every morning, except Sundays, a brougham would cross the Common with Peter Jones as its passenger on the way to his shop on Sloane Square.

Chelsea Creek

The Creek, now the site of Chelsea Harbour (*qv*), is the outlet of a river called Counters Creek or Billingwell Ditch. This rises in the grounds of Kensal Green Cemetery and receives a few short tributaries on its south-south-east route to the Thames.

30. *Chelsea Creek and Stanley Bridge near the King's Road. Drawing by Walter Greaves.*

Just as the Westbourne marks Chelsea's eastern boundary, so the Creek is the western limit.

Before industrialisation the Creek had many attractions, enough anyway to warrant the building of two substantial houses on its banks – Stanley House on the Chelsea side of the river, just north of the King's Road, and Sands End on the Fulham side, once the home of Joseph Addison (qv), who described the larks and nightingales in the vicinity.

In 1828 an economically disastrous project, instigated by the 2nd Earl of Kensington, canalised Counters Creek for two miles south from Counters Bridge in Kensington High Street. The new waterway was 100 feet wide and able to carry vessels of 100 tons burden. The aim, for this first stage, was to offload goods in Kensington, take them to the Thames on the canal and then offload again on to Thames barges – and vice versa, of course. The eventual aim was to have the canal go north of Kensington High Street to connect with the Grand Union Canal at Paddington.

On 12 August 1828 the principal participants in the scheme took a barge at Battersea Bridge and proceeded up the canal 'amidst cheers of the multitude assembled' and were fortified at the other end by a sumptuous dinner.

But by the mid 1830s the scheme was described as 'a total failure' and the plans for its extension to Paddington were abandoned. It must have been with some relief, therefore, that the proprietors sold out the route to the promoters of a new railway, the Birmingham, Bristol & Thames Junction. This line connected to the Great Western at Willesden in the north and was constructed down to the old canal basin south of Kensington High Street– fr om 'nowhere to nowhere' was the wry description – and it was no wonder that the railway, like the canal, failed. Its fortunes revived only when it was extended further south along the bed of the canal to cross the Thames at Chelsea Creek and join a number of lines in Battersea. Even then the railway fared badly and has only in recent years assumed a new strategic importance.

The railway and the canal inevitably attracted industry to this low-lying, unwanted area of Chelsea. The largest enterprise was the Imperial Gas Works on the Fulham side of the Creek, pouring out its smoke and effluent on to Chelsea, but there were many factories on the Chelsea side including the Cadogan Iron Works and a timber mill and brewery in Dudmaston House and its grounds. In 1892 the Chelsea historian, Alfred Beaver, wrote that 'The Creek is now a dirty ditch lined with ugly wharves and sheds, railway engines dashing past constantly and a wilderness of more or less dingy streets covers the farmlands and gardens'.

31. The demolition of Duke Street in 1873. The street ran parallel to the Thames and was, in effect, a continuation of the line of Cheyne Walk. The destruction of the south side is being watched from the north (see Chelsea Embankment overleaf).

34. *Alldin's Coal Wharf and Arch House; extract from a drawing by Walter Greaves.*

32. *Looking west down Duke Street, from Danvers Street.*

Chelsea Embankment

The early heart of Chelsea was by the riverside on each side of Old Church Street. The development of King's Road in the 19th century, and the building of a new parish church of St Luke in Sydney Street in 1824 confirmed a gradual move of the village northwards. Much of the charm of Chelsea, however, still remained by the riverside, where wharves, old inns, shops and houses were picturesque and beloved of artists. This scene had a rude awakening.

In its determination to improve the drainage and sewerage of London, the Metropolitan

33. *Looking east from Danvers Street, along Lombard Street. Drawing by Walter Greaves.*

Board of Works embarked on the massive construction of the embankment of the Thames. The Victoria Embankment between Blackfriars and Westminster Bridge was opened in 1870, and the Albert Embankment from Westminster to Vauxhall in the same year. The logical extension to this work was the Chelsea Embankment which resulted in a widened Cheyne Walk, from the Royal Hospital to Battersea Bridge. This was formally opened on 9 May, 1874. Though Chelsea residents may have bemoaned the intrusion of the nineteenth century, the embankment at Chelsea was vital. Not only did it contain improvements to the sanitation of the area but it was a barrier to the rising level of the river.

A particular loss was Lombard Street and its continuation Duke Street, which ran parallel to the river, between Old Church Street on the east and Beaufort Street on the west, with Danvers Street entering in the middle (see illustrations 31-3). Lombard Street was, in effect, an extension of Cheyne Walk, and was entered through the arch of a building called Arch House, otherwise known as Alldin's Coal Wharf – it is shown in ill. 34. Most likely the coal delivered here in the first half of the nineteenth century came from the Midlands via the canal system to Brentford, where it was offloaded into Thames boats.

Chelsea Flower Show

The annual flower show staged by the Royal Horticultural Society was first held in the grounds of the Royal Hospital in May 1913. Previously it had been staged in the grounds of the Inner Temple, but relations between the gardeners and the lawyers became difficult after a

35. *The Chelsea football team in 1905.*

time. It was appropriate, in any case, that the Show moved to Chelsea, for not only was there more room, but one of the founders of the RHS, William Forsyth, was a one-time curator of the Physic Garden.

Chelsea Football Club

The founders of the Club were Gus and Joe Mears, owners of a constructional engineers' business responsible for building the Fulham river embankment. In 1904 they leased the site of the old London Athletic Club beside the West London Railway line, between Lillie Road and Fulham Road – it is now called Stamford Bridge and the Club is actually in Fulham, rather than Chelsea.

Chelsea joined the Football League in 1905 and by the 1906/7 season were in the First Division, when a crowd of 60,000 watched them play Manchester United.

Chelsea's trophy cupboard, however, remained obstinately bare until 1954/5 when they won the League, and they did not win the FA Cup until 1970, with further wins in 1997 and 2000. They went on to win the European Cup Winners' Cup in 1971 and 1998 and the Football League Cup was won in 1965 and 1998.

Notable players have included Tommy Lawton, Roy Bentley,

Peter Bonetti and Ray Wilkins.

Of recent years many of the team squad have been signed from overseas. In the summer of 2003 the then owner of the club, Ken Bates, unexpectedly sold out to a Russian billionaire, Roman Abramovich, who then embarked upon a spectacularly expensive spree of player signing.

Chelsea Harbour

The Chelsea Harbour development is, like a number of enterprises with Chelsea in their name, not in Chelsea. As described under Chelsea Creek (qv), the area was a desolate one, degraded by years of aggressive industrialisation and one in which only the poor would seek a home.

36. *Chelsea Harbour.*

37. The Chelsea Hospital for Women.

So unwanted was the area that in 1965, when the new London boroughs were being formulated, the putative Hammersmith & Fulham Council, aware that the area would be a constant drain on its resources, proposed that it be taken over by the new Kensington & Chelsea borough. The latter swiftly declined, for this land held little prospect of improvement. So, the site remained in Hammersmith & Fulham, which, once Chelsea Harbour was built, has received the considerable rate income from the premises.

The project was the idea of architect Ray Moxley. In the 1980s the 20 acres or so were bought by P & O and Globe so that 'a unique world of houses, flats, offices, restaurants and shops and a luxury hotel built around a working yacht harbour' could be erected. Its architecture is post-modernist, and a riverside walk for the public has been created.

Chelsea Hospital for Women

This hospital, founded in 1871, was housed in a handsome redbrick building at 78 King's Road in 1883. It later moved to Dovehouse Street and was eventually incorporated into Queen Charlotte's Hospital at Stamford Brook.

38. Chelsea House in Cadogan Place, the London home of the Cadogan family.

Chelsea House

Chelsea House was the London residence of the Cadogan family. In its earlier days it was situated on the site of the Duke of York Square redevelopment in King's Road. Its most recent manifestation was at the eastern end of the northern terrace of Cadogan Place, a huge building with a dining room measuring 44 feet x 21 feet. There were 21 rooms for the family plus servants' quarters in basement and attics. When the family was there, usually just for three months a year, thirty staff attended them.

Chelsea House was demolished in 1935 and flats now occupy its site.

Chelsea Library

Enthusiasm for the provision of public libraries emerged in the 1850s, but in London there was a great deal of resistance to the idea. Not only would libraries increase the rate burden but those who were entitled to vote on the matter were reluctant to subsidise books, especially fiction, which would be enjoyed by

the poorer classes. To his credit the 5th Earl Cadogan was an influential advocate of the public library campaign.

Vestries wishing to introduce public libraries, based on the expenditure of a 1d in the £1 rate, could do so only after a public referendum of those ratepayers entitled to vote, which was usually accompanied by heated public meetings. Many vestries did not adopt the Library Act legislation when campaigning was at its height in the 1880s, and some had hardly begun to consider the matter before vestries were abolished in 1900 and London boroughs were established: these had no need to call referendums on the matter.

In Chelsea the familiar battle between ratepayers and liberal campaigners developed. A poster printed in 1887 by 'A Ratepayer' asked voters to consider the poor tradesmen 'who sell and lend Newspapers and Novels' who would lose business by the introduction of libraries, and of course, 'the oppressive burden of your Rates

39. Lord Cadogan laying the foundation stone of Chelsea Library in Manresa Road, on 8 February 1890. The architect, J M Brydon, is to the right of the man with the top hat and moustache in the bottom right hand part of the picture.

increased'. The victorious pro-library campaigners, led by vestryman Benjamin Findon, had on their side Cadogan, two lords and the Rector of Chelsea.

The first Chelsea library opened in two rooms temporarily fitted up in the old Vestry Hall in the King's Road. Shortly after this a site was made available by Cadogan in Manresa Road, together with a gift of £300 to buy technical books. J M Brydon designed the building, which opened on 8 February 1890. The first librarian, John Quinn, also began the invaluable archive of local material that is now such a pleasure to sift through. He was also the first librarian in London to provide a special study room for children.

In September 1940 the library was devastated by fire and it did not reopen fully until 1951. Even worse, in the view of many Chelsea residents, it was transferred to part of Chelsea Town Hall after the merger of the borough into Kensington & Chelsea.

Chelsea Manor Houses

The first Chelsea Manor House was located at the northern end of today's Lawrence Street. Sir Reginald Bray owned the manor from 1485 to 1503, and was succeeded by his nephew Sir Edmund, Lord Bray, who surrendered the property in 1510 to Sir William Sandys. Both the Brays were buried in the Old Church. Sandys exchanged the house and manor with Henry VIII for property in Hampshire, and the king built a new manor house facing the river in what is now Cheyne Walk in 1543. Meanwhile the older house was tenanted and in 1583 it came into the possession of Thomas Lawrence, a goldsmith, from whom Lawrence Street is named. He died in 1593 and was buried in a medieval chapel in the Old Church, which thereafter was called the Lawrence Chapel.

By the early 18th century the older manor house appears to have been demolished and the site taken by several houses, one of which was occupied by the widow of James, Duke of Monmouth; this became known as Monmouth House. The duchess had begun life as Anne Scott and was Countess of Bucchleuch in her own right. In 1663 she was married to James, an illegitimate son of Charles II, when he was only 14 years old; in that same year he was made Duke of Monmouth.

Monmouth, when older, had aspirations to the throne. Charles II had no legitimate male heir and his brother, who became James II, was not popular in

40. *Monmouth House at the northern end of Lawrence Street.*

England, partly because he was Catholic. Monmouth was persuaded to take his chance upon the death of Charles II and led the so-called Monmouth Rebellion in 1685. For his part in this Monmouth was executed at the Tower.

We know that in 1716 the Princess Caroline of Anspach, the future Queen of England (wife of George II), visited the duchess at Chelsea, and the parish registers record that six shillings were paid to the bellringers at the church on that occasion.

The duchess died in 1732 and the next tenant of note in Monmouth House was the novelist Tobias Smollett, who came with his wife and child in 1749. He was still there in 1757, but had left by 1763. Contemporary with Smollett in part of the property was Nicholas Sprimont, who ran the Chelsea Porcelain factory (*qv*) adjacent. In 1815 all or part of Monmouth House was occupied by a boarding school run by a Mrs Pilsbury, though the house seems to have been entirely demolished in 1835.

Henry VIII's manor house was to the east side of today's Oakley Street, in the vicinity of nos. 19-26 Cheyne Walk. The house was seized by the State in 1653, after the Civil War, and sold off. Then, it was described as having three cellars, three halls, three parlours, three kitchens, another two parlours and nine other rooms, on the ground floor alone. On the next floor it had three drawing rooms, seventeen chambers and four closets, and summer rooms with a bedroom. This appears to include the property to the west, Winchester House (*qv*). The young Edward VI and Elizabeth I were housed here for part of their childhoods, together with the last of Henry's wives, Catherine Parr, with occasional visits from the unfortunate Jane Grey, then a girl of eleven. Later residents included the widows of both the Lord Protector Somerset (who was executed 1552) and the Duke of Northumberland, executed for his plan to put Jane Grey on the throne instead of Mary. Also in the household, until her death in 1557, was another of Henry's discarded wives, Anne of Cleves.

It was this manor house that was taken by Sir Hans Sloane in 1742, and where he lived until his death in 1753. It was his in-

tention that his great collection of antiquities and natural history specimens should be housed at Chelsea, but it was eventually to form one of the founding collections of the British Museum in Bloomsbury. The house and its grounds thus came on to the market at a time when development along the Chelsea riverfront was an attractive proposition, and the house was demolished in 1755.

David Le Lay, in the 2002 *Chelsea Society Annual Report* has identified another house which was called Manor House. This was built in 1780 by Thomas Richardson, facing east along present-day St Leonard's Terrace. It was demolished in 1870.

Chelsea Old Church

The first mention of a church at Chelsea is found in a Papal taxation document of 1290, though it is likely that one existed by 1157. The early building was known as All Saints and later as St Luke's – it reverted to All Saints, but more commonly Chelsea Old Church, when the new parish church of St Luke was built in Sydney Street in 1821.

The church will forever be associated with Sir Thomas More (*qv*), who lived in a house on the site of Beaufort Street (*qv*) before his imprisonment and execution by Henry VIII in 1535. He rebuilt the south-east chapel in the church in 1528 for his own private worship, and his tomb is still in the building.

The church was 'much decayed' in 1667 and it was, even by then, too small for the growing population, since 'divers great and noble personages' had moved into the district, doubtless buying up the pews in the church, so that the 'many ancient inhabitants and families' were finding themselves too often excluded from worship.

After the Restoration the church was altered – the tower was replaced, the windows enlarged, new pews installed and an extension made. A new roof was paid for by Lady Jane Cheyne. At the time the new tower, at 113ft, was the highest brick-built edifice in the country. However, it did reverberate when the bells were rung and had to be strengthened on a number of occasions.

Disaster came in 1941. On the night of 16/17 April, 450 German bombers combined to blitz London. Eighteen hospitals and thirteen churches were hit, one of which was Chelsea Old Church, which was reduced to a shell.

A booklet was published in 1957, in aid of the rebuilding fund, which told the story of that night, when the southern end of Old Church Street was devastated. All but one of the fire watchers for this area were

42. Chelsea Old Church in 1908.

killed and many other people injured.

'The South end of Old Church Street presented a scene of desolation; the tower of the Old Church had come down and the street was blocked by a confusion of bricks and rubble, which extended over all the site of the Old Church. The Sanctuary stood open to the weather, the beautiful altar rails were broken and the altar and Cross were severely damaged by a fallen beam. The More tomb was in pieces; the Bray Tomb,

41. Chatelaine's south-east view of the Old Church in 1750.

43. *A scene of devastation after a landmine destroyed Chelsea Old Church in 1941.*

protected by its arch, remained... Yet, rising out of all this ruin, there – almost incredibly – stood the More chapel, the pillars with the Holbein capitals, supporting the arch, intact, unscathed. It seemed to hold a faint promise for the future.'

Fortunately, the antiquarian and architectural expert, Walter Godfrey, was on hand (he had been responsible for the *Survey of London* volumes on Chelsea), and much of the damaged rubble was sensitively preserved.

After the war, there was much discussion as to whether the church should be rebuilt and if so, in what form. It should be remembered that the Church of England had many calls on its funding at that time, because of wartime damage, and the proposal to rebuild Chelsea Old Church was not a high priority. But the church's acknowledged historical importance could not be dismissed lightly. However, the decision to recreate the church in a similar form, using as much as could be rescued from the damaged remains, was a brave one given the lack of resources in the 1950s.

While building work contin-

ued the More Chapel and the Lawrence Chapel were used for services. The church was rededicated by the Bishop of London in 1958.

Monuments which survived the bombing include that to Lord and Lady Dacre, who lived in Sir Thomas More's old home in the 1590s: Lady Anne lies in marble finery beside her bearded husband who is in soldier's armour. The Bray family, the oldest we know of in Chelsea, still have their monument though it is largely unreadable, and Lady Jane Cheyne has a life-size recumbent figure. The Duchess of Northumberland, who died in 1555, a year after the execution of her husband for his part in the plot to put Lady Jane Grey on the throne, has a monument in the south-east corner. A memorial to Thomas Lawrence (1598), after whose family Lawrence Street is named, is also preserved. One of the grandest monuments is that of Sir Robert Stanley.

Modern memorials include those for the artist William de Morgan (*qv*), and Henry James (*qv*). The font of 1673 survives, though its cover is a reproduc-

tion. The six chained books, the only ones in any London church, were a gift of Sir Hans Sloane, who is buried in the churchyard.

Chelsea Palace

The Chelsea Palace of Varieties, as it was first called, opened on 13 April 1903, at 232-242 King's Road. Its architects were Wylson and Lang, and it had seating for just over 2,500. Dramatically, the Palace did not have a distinguished career, for it seems to have kept to music hall entertainment, staging the likes of George Robey, Vesta Tilley, 'Wee' Georgie Wood and Gracie Fields, and like most theatres of its kind, it relied very heavily on the income from the annual pantomime. The Palace declined rapidly after the Second World War despite the introduction of a non-titillating mixture of circus and nudity.

The theatre closed in 1957 and was bought by Granada for a recording studio. It was demolished in the 1950s. Heal's shop is now on the site.

Chelsea Park

Lord Wharton's Chelsea Park is shown on Hamilton's map of 1677 and its area is quite easy to pick out on modern maps. It lay between Fulham Road and King's Road, its western boundary being today's Park Walk by the well-known kink in the King's Road, and its eastern boundary was Old Church Street.

Park Walk, previously called Lovers Walk, was built at the end of the 18th century and the rest, including the northern extension of Beaufort Street, followed piecemeal. Chelsea Park Gardens and Elm Park Road are some of the reminders of the old 40-acre estate.

44. *Chelsea Palace in the King's Road, c.1904.*

45. *A woman and child, a figurine made at the Chelsea works.*

Chelsea Polytechnic

The Regent Street Polytechnic, founded by Quintin Hogg in 1882, had a number of consequences elsewhere. One of them is today's University of Westminster in Marylebone Road. Chelsea too was affected by Hogg's pioneering. With the aid of a grant from the City Parochial Charities, and a site donated by the Cadogan Estate, the South Western Polytechnic was built in Manresa Road. It majored heavily on 'productive' subjects, those suitable for skilled artisans, and even those who wanted 'preparation for colonial life'. The name was changed in 1922 to the Chelsea Polytechnic and by then the courses included pharmacy and chiropody.

There have been many changes since the last war as successive governments have altered and re-altered the status and functions of educational establishments. The College founded a campus in Wandsworth in a link with St George's Hospital Medical School, and in 1985 Chelsea College became part of King's College. this in turn has been moving out of Manresa Road in recent years.

Chelsea Porcelain

One of the more profitable imports of the East India Trading Company during the seventeenth century was porcelain from China. It surpassed anything previously seen in England and no home-grown manufacturer could match its delicate design and transluscence. John Dwight in Fulham produced something approaching it in the 1670s, but it simply wasn't as good. A breakthrough came in 1745 when superb porcelain was made in Chelsea under, it is thought, the auspices of Sir Everard Fawkener. The *Daily Advertiser* of 5 March that year noted that 'We hear that China made at Chelsea is arriv'd to such Perfection, as to equal if not surpass the finest old Japan, allow'd so by the most approv'd Judges here.'

The enterprise was taken over by a French silversmith, Nicholas Sprimont. He was sufficiently successful to build a purpose-built factory in Lawrence Street on the corner of today's Justice Walk in 1750 and to sell it at the Chelsea China Warehouse in St James's Street in the West End. His range included Japanese,

Chinese and classical scenes. Some of the workforce, like Sprimont himself, were Huguenots, who had fled persecution in France. One of his workers, William Duesbury, specialised in figurines, such as bird models – in 1756 he left Sprimont and began his own business in Derby. The firm also made snuff boxes, scent bottles and pill cases. About 1749 Joseph Willems, a Belgian, arrived. He too specialised in figure models.

A number of maker's marks were incised on Chelsea porcelain, but most often it was a Red Anchor, which today is the symbol of the Chelsea Society.

The corpulent Sprimont's health did not match his enthusiasm, and when he was too ill to continue with the enterprise he sold it off in 1769 to a James Cox who then sold it on to Duesbury, still then in Derby. A 1772 sale by Christie's advertised 'the last year's produce of the Derby and Chelsea Porcelaine Manufactory'. It was about that year that the number of employees, which in the

46. *Figures of birds made at Chelsea.*

firm's heyday had been around 100, plus boys from charity and pauper schools, had fallen to seven, with a horse operating the machinery. Within a few years the site of the factory had been cleared and Duesbury had retired to Derby.

The site of the factory is now marked by a plaque and the nearby Red Anchor Close.

Chelsea Reach

This stretch of the Thames is to the east of Battersea Bridge, from Beaufort Street to the east of the Royal Hospital. It is one of the most attractive stretches of the urban Thames, with the Hospital, the Physic Garden and Cheyne Walk to the north, and Battersea Park to the south.

Chelsea Rectory

The Rectory in Old Church Street was built *c.*1725 and much extended while still in church hands. An immensely valuable site (with two acres of gardens), it was sold into private hands in the 1980s and the house has been very expensively enlarged even more since.

The garden, one of the largest in central London, was originally about 14 acres.

Rectors have included William Cadogan, who was happy to have John Wesley in his pulpit, Dr Gerald Wellesley, the brother of the Duke of Wellington, Charles Kingsley, father of two notable authors, Charles and Henry Kingsley, and the Rev. Gerald Blunt, father of Chelsea historian Reginald Blunt.

Chelsea Society

The Chelsea Society was formed on 1 April 1927 to 'protect and foster' the amenities of Chelsea. It began at a meeting held in a drawing room at Wentworth House, Swan Walk, the residence of Mary, Countess of Lovelace. It was the enthusiasm of Reginald Blunt (*qv*), son of a Chelsea rector, that made its formation possible and he devoted much of the last seventeen years of his long life to the affairs of the Society.

The Society was formed at an opportune moment when significant developments were occurring in Chelsea, but much of its best work has taken place in modern times when a period of very high property prices and a retailing boom has trans-

47. Chelsea Rectory between the wars.

heritage, the result of a competition held in 1912. The borough council in 1914 decided to erase the literary mural because it contained a portrait of the 'disgraced' Oscar Wilde – it also included George Eliot and the venerable Thomas Carlyle – but the advent of war delayed matters and this censorship was never carried out.

The building's use as an administrative Town Hall was abandoned after the creation of the borough of Kensington & Chelsea in 1965 and the opening of the new town hall complex in Kensington. Its principal use now is for recreation, a registry office and Chelsea Library.

Chelsea College of Art

The present college, partly based in Manresa Road, is an amalgamation of the art school that began within the Chelsea Polytechnic and the West London School of Art in Great Titchfield Street. Henry Moore and Graham Sutherland were both teachers here.

The Chelsea College is now part of the London Institute. In

formed what was once an informal, sometimes slightly shabby area into a very smart and exploited part of London. In the 1960s when many old buildings in London were demolished without too much public outcry, the Society was very active, in particular against an insensitive plan of the Cadogan Estate to erect two 33-storey blocks in the neighbourhood of Tedworth Square.

Mr Blunt at the inaugural meeting said that the purpose of the Society should be to organize so that 'with great tact and guidance, with all due respect to the rights of owners and public authorities, and after careful examination of all the circumstances' to prevent 'irreparable destruction' and 'obnoxious construction'. The fight goes on.

The address of the Society is 4 Cranley Place, SW7 3AB.

Chelsea Town Hall

A Chelsea Vestry Hall was built on garden ground in the King's Road in 1858, together with a public baths and a Scientific Institution. It was completed at

the beginning of March 1861, the work of the architect W Pocock. In 1887 a new hall was built at the rear of the old one, fronting Manor Gardens, designed by J M Brydon. In 1908 the original Vestry Hall was demolished and the present hall, facing King's Road, was built, incorporating the 1887 building. It was designed by Leonard Stokes. Inside are murals emphasising Chelsea's artistic, literary and scientific

48. The first Chelsea Vestry/Town Hall.

December 2000 it was announced that the disparate parts of the College (it is at three other sites in west London) will be consolidated at the former Royal Army Medical College next to Tate Britain on Millbank.

The Chelsea Theatre

This was established, as the Chelsea Theatre Centre, in 1992 in the World's End development under the artistic direction of Francis Alexander. The building has recently been refurbished and reopened in September 2003 with a programme of new works.

Chelsea Waterworks Company

John Evelyn noted in his diary in May 1696 a visit to Chelsea: 'I made my Lord Cheney a visit at Chelsea, and saw those ingenious water-works invented by Mr Winstanley [architect of the Eddystone lighthouse], wherein were some things very surprising and extraordinary.' This was not, however, an early water supply for the area, but an invention related to fountains.

In 1723 the Chelsea Waterworks Company was incorporated, although its engine house and works were actually outside the parish border, east of the Westbourne river, roughly where the Grosvenor railway bridge crosses the Thames. Its main remit was to supply Westminster with water, though Chelsea derived some dubious benefit from its supply. Various reservoirs were constructed including one on the site of the later Victoria Station, one in Hyde Park opposite Mount Street and another in Green Park, near Piccadilly just opposite today's underground station. Eventually the Company's numerous cuts and channels north of the Thames extended over 89 acres of today's Pimlico. At first water was raised from the lower levels by waterwheels and horse-operated machinery, but in 1742 the first economically successful steam pumping engine was erected on the site of today's Grosvenor Hotel.

The water, collected directly and unfiltered from the Thames was highly polluted, despite its supply to a prestigious clientele. Tobias Smollett, a Chelsea resident at about this time, noted that the water was 'impregnated with all the filth of London and Westminster, of which human excrement is the least offensive'. And in 1827, well after filtering had commenced, Sir Francis Burdett claimed in Parliament that 'the water taken up below Chelsea Hospital and London Bridge was charged with the contents of more than 130 common sewers as well as the drainings from dung hills, refuse from hospitals, lead, gas and soap works' – indeed there was a white lead works very close to the Chelsea pumping station.

At first water was conveyed in hollowed-out tree trunks, but in 1746 the Company laid iron pipes from the Thames to Hyde Park. Sand filtration was introduced in 1829 but Parliament at long last in 1852 restricted the intake from the Thames to above Teddington Lock. By that time the Company was supplying well over 13,000 houses.

49. *The works of the Chelsea Water Company on the Thames in 1752.*

The Company shifted its location in 1856 when a new intake, filter beds and a pumping station were installed at Surbiton; from there the supply went to a reservoir on Putney Heath and then by gravitation to the Company's area of supply on the north side of the Thames. In 1877 the supply came from West Molesey.

The Metropolitan Water Board took over the Company's operations in 1904.

Chelsea Yachts

On the Thames where Lots Road runs into Cheyne Walk is the Chelsea Yacht and Boat Company, using a part of the river which from the earliest times has been a scene of boats and wharves. Before the Embankment the area was a busy one, portrayed in the paintings of the Greaves brothers (qv) and in the photographs of James Hedderley (qv). At the eastern end of the present moorings the father of the Greaves brothers owned a boatyard and it was he who ferried J M W Turner to wherever the artist wanted. At the western end was a coal wharf.

The Chelsea Yacht and Boat Company was founded here in 1935 by Charles Fleming, mainly as a boat repair place, though some mooring space was kept. During the last war the firm became contractors to the Admiralty and naval launches and barges were built. Vessels went from here to join in the 'little ships' evacuation from Dunkirk in 1940 and other vessels were used in the Normandy invasion in 1944. Peacetime required a new function to make the enterprise economic and gradually houseboat moorings, stimulated by the shortage of more conventional housing, have tended to dominate.

The Company is now run by Peter Osgood, whose father had taken over after the death of Fleming.

The Chenil Galleries

The former Chenil Galleries at 181/183 King's Road originated as a meeting place of artists at Charles Chenil's art materials shop in the 1890s. It developed into a gallery in 1905 devised by John Knewstub, whose father had worked for Rossetti and whose sisters were married to William Orpen and William Rothenstein. The gallery became the hub of the Chelsea art world, with one room devoted to a standing collection, and another housing temporary exhibitions. From 1910 Augustus John had a studio here, and other artists associated with the venture were Mark Gertler, Eric Gill and Roger Fry. David Bomberg had his first one-man show at Chenil in July 1914, when he exhibited 55 pictures, which caused the *Daily Chronicle* to claim that those who visited such shows were not the public but 'youthful, eager artists with strange hats and strong opinions'.

In the same year the galleries staged the first solo show by the sculptor Frank Dobson.

The galleries were relaunched, (with Augustine Birrell officiating), in 1925 and the next few years or so were their heyday, for they staged more than visual arts.

In *c.*1926 the young John Barbirolli conducted his own chamber orchestra here, and John Drinkwater gave poetry readings. William Walton's *Façade* was staged on 27 and 29 June 1926, with the Sitwells and Diaghilev present. Gwen John had her only solo exhibition at the Chenil in 1926. But the heyday was short and the receivers were called in. In 1933, when the space was being let out, Duke Ellington and his orchestra recorded here for Decca. At the outbreak of war the premises were used for Civil Defence. Afterwards the building was sold to the council and local art exhibitions were held there, as well as X-ray sessions. In 1977 the galleries became privately owned again and were usually used to sell antiques.

The building is now occupied by a toy shop and the interior, except the staircases, has little to remind us of the former splendour.

50. The Chenil Galleries, 2003.

The Cheyne Centre

The Centre began in June 1875 as the Cheyne Hospital for Children. Founded by a Mr and Mrs Wickham Flower, it was located at 46 Cheyne Walk. Its aim was to take children suffering from chronic disease who would otherwise be excluded from general hospitals. In effect, the hospital specialised in cerebral palsy. It soon expanded into 5 houses in Cheyne Walk and then rebuilt them as the Chelsea Hospital for Spastic Children in 1889. The building has more recently been converted into apartments.

The Hospital, which for many years had facilities outside London, has now moved some of its operations to the Chelsea and Westminster Hospital in Fulham Road, and others to West Wickham in Kent.

Cheyne Row

Cheyne Row is one of the oldest streets in Chelsea. Some houses were built soon after William

Cheyne inherited the manor of Chelsea in 1698 – a row of houses on the west side, built in 1703, survives. The road is chiefly known for Carlyle House, where Thomas Carlyle lived from 1834 to 1881 (*qv*), but there is another plaque (a private one) to Margaret Daimer Dawson, pioneer of women in the police force, at no. 10. The artist, Glyn Philpot, had a studio at 14a in 1906-9. The potter and tile-maker, William de Morgan, lived at no. 30 and had a studio on the site of the Church of Our Most Holy Redeemer.

The church, designed by Edward Goldie, was opened in 1905. On the altar is a relic from Sir Thomas More's vertebrae, which came from the convent in Bruges where his adopted daughter, Margaret Clements,

became a nun. The church was bombed in September 1940 when about 100 people were sheltering there – 19 lost their lives.

Cheyne Walk

This most elegant stretch of London's riverside extends from Flood Street in the east to Cremorne Walk on the west. Starting from the eastern end, nos 1-26 are built on the grounds and site of the second Chelsea manor house, erected by Henry VIII; nos 27-45 (and including Oakley Street) are on the grounds and sites of Winchester House on the east and Shrewsbury House on the west.

A good many of the original houses in the Walk survive, although many alterations, exter-

51. No. 72 Cheyne Walk.

52. The Thames Coffee House and The Cricketers pub, on the site of Carlyle Mansions in Cheyne Walk.

nal and internal, have been made. Those interested in the fine detail of these are recommended to read the *Survey of London, The Parish of Chelsea*, vol. II (1909) available at Chelsea Local History Library.

Some of the older properties and a good number of the illustrious residents of this street are noted here.

No. 1 was rebuilt 1887-88 on the site of an early 18th-century house, but it does contain some features from other old houses in the vicinity. The prominent actor-manager, Seymour Hicks (1871-1949), lived here in 1937.

No. 2, is c.1717, refronted in 1879. The actor John Barrymore (1882-1942) lived here 1924-5.

No. 3 was built c.1717. Residents have included Sir John Goss (1800-1880), who lived here while organist at the Old Church. He was here again when he was appointed organist at St Paul's Cathedral. A later resident (1840-51) was Admiral William Henry Smith (1788-1865), Vice President of the Royal Society and a founder of the Royal Geographical Society. This house was acquired in 1942 by the National Trust to house the Benton Fletcher collection of musical instruments, which are now at Fenton House in Hampstead.

No. 4, which has a particularly attractive doorway, was built c.1718. Residents have included the artists William Dyce (1846-7) and Daniel Maclise (1861-70), and the writer George Eliot, in 1880, who died within a few weeks of moving in.

No. 5, also built c.1718, was the home of the Neild family – *see James Camden Neild*.

No. 6 was built c.1718 for Joseph Danvers. A later resident was Dr Dominiceti (*qv*), as from 1765. The composer, Sir Arthur Sullivan (1842-1900), was here as a boy.

No. 10 was the residence in 1924-5 of the former prime minister, David Lloyd George.

The composer Ralph Vaughan Williams (1872-1958), was at *No. 13* from 1905 until 1929.

Nos 15-18 were all built c.1717. The largest, Queen's House, at no. 16, is so named from a misconception that it was once occupied by Catherine of Braganza. Dante Gabriel Rossetti (*qv*) was here for nearly 20 years from 1862. His lodgers included his brother William and the poet, Algernon Swinburne. Rossetti also had peacocks in the garden, much to the annoyance of neighbours.

The musician and composer, Thomas Attwood (1783-1856), a pupil of Mozart (*qv*) and later organist of St Paul's Cathedral, lived (and died) at no. 17.

No.18 became the well-

53. *Looking upstream from Cheyne Walk in the 18th century.*

known coffee house of Don Saltero *(qv)*.

Nos 19-26 were built on the site of Henry VIII's manor house itself in the early 1750s. The writer Percy Wyndham Lewis (1882-1957), was at *no. 21* in 1935-6.

Walter Greaves, the Chelsea artist (1846-1930), was born at *no. 31*. *No. 37* was on the site of the old public house called the Magpie and Stump *(qv)*, which itself was replaced by a house of that name built by the arts-and-crafts architect C R Ashbee *(qv)* in 1894; this, alas, was lost to redevelopment in 1968, but his other houses, nos. 38-39, survive.

Nos 43-45 are on the site of Shrewsbury House *(qv)*, and were built in the early 18th century.

Nos 46-48 (now two houses) were originally three separate dwellings, built *c*.1711 on the site of the Three Tuns, whose bowling green is occupied by part of Cheyne Row.

The Feathers was at the corner of Cheyne Row and Cheyne Walk – *no. 49* is now on its site.

The King's Head and Eight Bells *(qv)*, on the western corner with Cheyne Row, is now an upmarket restaurant called La Chaumiere.

The artist William Holman Hunt was at *no. 59* from 1850-3.

Nos 62-3, just east of the Old Church, were formerly part of a terrace of five properties called Church Row or Prospect Place. These were built *c*.1686 when Thomas Lawrence owned them.

Dr Francis Atterbury *(qv)* was at *no. 63*, as was Nicholas Sprimont in 1755-6, proprietor of the Chelsea Porcelain factory *(qv)* in Lawrence Street. The architect C R Ashbee *(qv)* lived at no. 74 – *see also Magpie and Stump*.

Carlyle Mansions were built in the 1880s, after the demolition of The Cricketers and the Thames Coffee House. These

54. *Looking east along Cheyne Walk c.1904.*

apartments have had more than their fair share of notable residents. They have included the composer Richard Addinsell (1904-77), at no. 1, Erskine Childers, the writer, (1870-1922), at no. 10, the poet T S Eliot (1888-1965) at no. 19 *c*.1915, the actor Gordon Harker (1885-1967) at no. 11, Henry James (1843-1916) at no. 21 from 1913, William Somerset Maugham (1874-1965) at no. 27 in 1904; another resident was the historian Arnold Toynbee (1889-1975).

Crosby Hall, dealt with separately, was transported from the City to the corner with Danvers Street.

Jacob Epstein (1880-1959), then a controversial sculptor, lived at *no. 72* before the First World War.

Nos 91-92 were built in 1771. The artist, Charles Conder (1868-1909), was at 91 in 1904.

The novelist, Elizabeth Gaskell, was born at *no. 93* in 1810 – her mother died within a week of the birth. The house, and *no. 94*, were built in 1777.

At *98-100* is Lindsey House – this is dealt with separately in this book.

The artist James Abbott McNeill Whistler lived at *no. 101*

when he first came to Chelsea in 1863-66. He was later to be found at no. 96 in 1866-78, no. 21 in 1890, and no. 74 in 1902-3.

No. 104 was the home of the Chelsea artist Walter Greaves (1846-1930) from 1855-97. His father owned a boat business on the riverfront here. The poet, Hilaire Belloc, was a resident in 1901-5, and *No. 109* was the home of the painter Philip Wilson Steer from 1898 until his death in 1942. A later resident was Cecil King, who owned the *Daily Mirror*.

J M W Turner *(qv)* lived at *No. 119*, as did the creator of the James Bond books, Ian Fleming in 1923-26.

Cinemas

The Chelsea Cinema at No. 206 King's Road opened *c*.1936 as the Gaumont. Only part of its auditorium is now used for films, the lower part being a Habitat shop. The UGC cinema on the corner of Old Church Street and King's Road, formerly the Essoldo, was once a skating rink. The Chelsea Classic cinema used to be on the western corner of Markham Street and the King's Road. What looks like an old cinema at No. 137 was in fact a Temperance Billiard Hall.

Thomas Crapper

Those who remember the 1960s' film, *The Servant*, with James Fox and Dirk Bogarde, may also recall in the early scenes a view of Thomas Crapper's premises at 120 King's Road. This usually raised some laughs as Crapper was well-known as a manufacturer and installer of flush toilets and other sanitary ware.

Crapper is often credited as being the inventor of the flush toilet, but he was not. He did, however, have a number of patents, ranging over water closets, pipe joints, drains and manhole covers – a number of the latter are installed within Westminster Abbey – and he did popularise decorated lavatory basins.

Crapper (1836-1910) came from Doncaster, where his brothers were dockers and his father a sailor. He walked to London when aged eleven, became an apprentice to a plumber in Sydney Street, and later began his own business. His works and first showroom were in what was then Marlborough Road (now Draycott Avenue). Crapper became a plumber to royalty, and was responsible for improvements at Sandringham and Windsor. He sold out to his partners in 1904. It was they who relocated the showroom to the King's Road. This closed in 1966. The company has in recent years been reformed to provide period-style sanitary ware.

There is no connection between Crapper the surname and 'crap' meaning defecate – the word in this sense was in use long before Crapper set up in business.

Cremorne Gardens

Cremorne Gardens was one of two significant pleasure grounds in Chelsea – Ranelagh was the other. Cremorne was later, some twenty years after its more famous predecessor had closed. Much of its site is today covered by the old Lots Road power station and the terraces around it.

Originally, the area was known as Chelsea Farm, once the home of the appallingly pious Countess of Huntingdon, founder of a Methodist sect. In 1778 the property was bought by one, Thomas Dawson who, seven years later, was created Viscount Cremorne. His wife was a great grand-daughter of William Penn (and named Philadelphia because of that). Upon her death the estate was bought by the self-styled Baron de Beaufain, *aka* Charles Randon de Berenger, who claimed to be a Prussian nobleman, but was in fact a fairly notorious fraudster. His plan for the estate was to establish a sporting club for men and women (a 'Stadium'). This opened in 1832, but as time went on more populist attractions, such as fireworks, circus and dancing took place, punctuated by balloon ascents. Shooting was popular, as was golf.

Cremorne Stadium was not a great success and by 1843 it was closed, but almost immediately reopened under the management of a larger-than-life character called Renton Nicholson who turned it into an even more

55. A scene in Cremorne Gardens.

56. The 'Female Blondin' crossing the Thames to Cremorne on a tightrope in August 1861. From the Illustrated London News.

spectacular, rather than a sporting, venue. The entrepreneurial spirit was continued by the next manager from 1846, Thomas Bartlett Simpson, once a waiter in Drury Lane, but now wealthy enough to embark on an enterprise that needed considerable investment – it is said that the opening celebration alone cost £5,000. He wanted to ape the Ranelagh Gardens, and to that end introduced theatre, dancing, concert rooms, gardens and grottos, mazes, circus performers and supper rooms.

The grounds consisted of twelve acres, abutting north on the King's Road and south on the river. Many visitors arrived by steamboats, alighting on to a specially built landing stage. There was a large orchestra surrounded by a dancing platform. Visitors were also entertained in a pagoda, Swiss chalets, bandstands, temples and a playhouse.

Spectacle was necessary to keep the crowds coming and the most popular attractions at

57. The ascent of the Montgolfier balloon from Cremorne.

Cremorne were balloon ascents, some of which resulted in loss of life. The most prolific balloonist of his time was Charles Green, whose 365th ascent was from Cremorne. In 1837 he ascended together with a lady and a leopard. A Madame Poitevin went up in 1852, mounted on a heifer; on landing it was found that the animal was very ill and had to be put down. The balloonist was prosecuted for animal cruelty and fined. On one occasion a monkey made the trip. Para-

chuting down from balloons became a familiar and hazardous occurrence. More bizarrely, Vincent de Groof in 1874 attempted to descend from a height of 500 feet assisted only by a pair of very large wings and an attachment to the balloon. He was killed when he landed in Sydney Street.

The Cremorne clientele also paid to go up in a tethered balloon, as far as 2,000 feet, although occasionally it broke loose and once the luckless passengers found themselves safely landed in Tottenham.

A later manager of the Cremorne, and one of its most successful, was a likeable rogue, E T Smith, who often hired a £1000 note for the day, so as to impress people when he casually took it out of his pocket.

One of the more remarkable events was in 1861, when Madame Genevieve (actually Selina Young), known as the 'Female Blondin', attempted to cross the Thames from Battersea to

58. *A view of the Thames Coffee House and the adjacent Cricketers pub, on the site of today's Carlyle Mansions. Drawing by Henry Greaves in 1860.*

Cremorne on a tightrope. It was nearly a disaster because someone cut the guy ropes supporting the tightrope in order to steal the lead weights. This was discovered when the lady was half way across the Thames, but she managed to swing her way down to the Thames, where she was picked up by boat.

Cremorne was not without its detractors, in particular Chelsea neighbours and more particularly Thomas Carlyle, who detested distracting noise. Chelsea Vestry was anxious to stop its licence on the grounds that Cremorne attracted loose people. A writer put it bluntly: 'Cremorne was never able to parade in the newspapers that array of fashionable and distinguished personages who last night visited Vauxhall.' It was not a place that 'ladies' were in the habit of visiting unescorted, unless 'in disguise and on the sly'.

In 1877 the place had deteriorated still further and its licence was withdrawn.

The Cricketers

This popular pub in Cheyne Walk was on the site of Carlyle Mansions, facing the river. It was one of the many drinking places patronised by the artist, George Morland (1763-1804) who, allegedly, instead of paying his bill, painted a new inn sign for the landlord. This was hung outside until 1824, when it was replaced by a copy. In the meantime the original was used by the landlord to decorate the drinking booths he ran at race courses.

Crosby Hall

Crosby Hall at the Cheyne Walk end of Danvers Street is an unlikely Chelsea house. It consists of the Hall – the surviving remnant of Crosby Place, a house erected in Bishopsgate in the City of London c.1466 – attached to a Tudorish structure erected in the 1920s and, more recently, mock-Tudor buildings, fronting the river introduced by the present owner.

The Bishopsgate house was built for Sir John Crosby, grocer and woolman, prominent in the affairs of the City. Richard, Duke of Gloucester (the later Richard III) was lodged in the mansion in 1483 when he heard of the murder of the princes in the Tower – a fact noted in Shakespeare's play about that much maligned monarch.

The house had a history of varied uses. It was a prison for Royalist supporters during the Civil War, was severely damaged during the Great Fire of 1666, was the headquarters for a short time of the East India Company and later a nonconformist meeting house for nearly 100 years. Much damage was done to what was left of it early in the 19th century when a firm of packers divided it into floors, but in the late 1830s the Hall was greatly restored – one of the earlier buildings in London to be treated with respect instead of destruction. In 1842 the hall was leased to the Crosby Hall Liter-

59. *The interior of Crosby Hall, as depicted in 1819.*

60. The street front of Crosby Hall in Bishopsgate.

61. A view of Lawrence Street and the Cross Keys public house by Walter Greaves.

ary Institute, from 1860 it was a wine store, and from 1868 a restaurant.

The house was bought by a bank in 1908, with demolition and redevelopment in mind. Though a campaign was waged to retain the house in situ, not enough money was raised for this to be done, and so the bank dismantled the Hall piece by piece, handing it over to the London County Council who presented it to the University and City Association of London. The pieces were then transported to Chelsea, to the corner of Danvers Street and Cheyne Walk, and then when funds were available partially enclosed by a new Tudor-style building erected in 1926/7. This became the headquarters and hostel of the British Federation of University Women.

The Hall is 69 feet long, 27 feet wide and 38 feet high, with an open timber roof.

It was appropriate to transplant the hall to Chelsea because Sir Thomas More, whose house was quite near the present site of Crosby Hall, owned the Bishopsgate mansion in 1532-4, though he does not appear to have lived there.

Until the break-up of the Greater London Council, Crosby Hall was at times open to the public. However, with minimal consultation, the London Residuary Body, an organisation set up by the government to sell off the assets of the GLC, sold Crosby Hall into private hands. The new owner has begun a hugely expensive building development here, which most people find sensitively done, adding more mock-Tudor buildings so as to complete a quadrangle around the old Hall. It is said that the present owner intends the building to serve as his mausoleum.

The Cross Keys

The picture of this old and pleasant pub in Lawrence Street, painted by Walter Greaves, probably c.1860, shows just how open the street was to the Thames at that time. Now, the river is much narrower and the wide embankment prevents an intimacy with the river.

62. Sir John Danvers.

Danvers House

Part of the grounds of Sir Thomas More's old house at Chelsea was purchased by Sir John Danvers (1588-1655) in 1622. He was a cultured man, a courtier of both James I and Charles I, and well-travelled. He had made the most extraordinary first marriage at the age of 20, when he wed a widow more than twice his age and already the mother of ten children, one of whom, George Herbert, would achieve some fame as a

63. *Reconstruction of Danvers House and its gardens, by David Le Lay (2001).*

64. Houses at the corner of Danvers Street in 1894, by Walter Burgess. On 77 Cheyne Walk was a tablet which said 'This is Danvers Street begun in ye year 1696 by Benjamin Stallwood'. After the bombing of 1941 this tablet was removed to the garden of Crosby Hall.

poet and hymn writer, Danvers is said to have 'loved her for her wit', but so also did the poet John Donne, who lodged with them frequently. When she died in 1627, Donne wept as he preached at her funeral in Chelsea Old Church. Danvers then married Elizabeth Dauntsey, who brought with her a country etate in Wiltshire where he laid out some elaborate gardens. He was a supporter of the Parliamentary cause during the Civil War and he was one of the signatories of Charles I's death warrant.

His house at Chelsea, which faced the river, with grounds stretching back to the King's Road (shown in David Le Lay's remarkable reconstruction at illustration 63), was one of the earliest examples of the Italian renaissance in England, much influenced by Palladio. The architect is unknown, but there is the inevitable possibility of Inigo Jones being involved, or perhaps Danvers himself. As David Le Lay points out in an article in the *Chelsea Society Annual Report* (2001), it was unusual in that the house and garden were conceived as a single design

Danvers died in time, for he would have been taken as a regicide at the Restoration. The house was occupied later by Lord John Robartes, whose flirtatious wife Laetitia is thought to have had an affair with the Duke of York. Robartes sent her off to the country 'to end her barrenness', and on her return she bore him five children, Laetitia survived her 'sour and cynical' husband, who died in 1685, and became the second wife of Charles Cheyne, lord of

Chelsea manor.

The last occupant of Danvers House appears to have been Thomas (later Marquis) Wharton (1648-1715), renowned in his youth as 'the greatest rake in England'. He did not improve with age. He was described as 'that most profligate, impious and shameless of men' and his second wife, whom he married in 1692, was thought to be 'a flattering, fawning, canting creature'.

Grand though Danvers House was, it did not last long. By the beginning of the next century it was in such a bad state that it was taken down and Danvers Street was constructed across it – some of the new houses on the western side of the street were themselves demolished to make way for the intrusion of Crosby House (*qv*).

65. *William de Morgan.*

66. *Charles Dilke*

Danvers Street

The street was developed upon the site of Danvers House (*see above*) and its grounds – building began in the early years of the 18th century. Jonathan Swift (1667-1745) lived in a house on the west side in 1711, and here wrote *Letters to Stella*. The most famous resident of the street, however, was Alexander Fleming (1881-1955), the discoverer of penicillin, who was at no. 20a from 1929 until his death.

William de Morgan

De Morgan (1839-1917) became the most famous creator of glazed tiles and pottery of his time. Closely associated with William Morris and the Liberty enterprise, he began with stained glass and then went on to ceramics, rediscovering the lustreware technique by which he was able to produce intense colours reminiscent of Arab and Italian majolica ware.

He moved to no. 30 Cheyne Row in 1872 and built a kiln in the garden. Needing larger premises he took on Orchard House in the same street for a pottery – the Church of Our Most Holy Redeemer is now on

its site. His ten years here were his most productive of tiles, creating much of his best work, including the tiles installed in Leighton House to complement the blue Islamic tiles in the Arab Hall. He also made tiles for luxury liners.

De Morgan had other talents – he was a competent painter and novelist, and claimed that he made more money from writing than from pottery. This is a remarkable claim since he didn't start writing novels until he was 67.

But his lasting fame is from the tiles made at Chelsea and from the beautiful lustreware pots he made at Merton Abbey (where he moved in 1882) and Fulham from 1886. At Fulham he made the tiles used in Ernest Debenham's house at 8 Addison Road, Kensington.

By that time, the de Morgans (he was married to the painter, Evelyn Pickering) had moved to The Vale off the King's Road. When his rambling house there was wanted for redevelopment he moved on to 127 Old Church Street, where he spent most of his time writing. He died at that address.

Charles Dilke

Charles Wentworth Dilke (1843-1911) was Chelsea's member of parliament from 1868 to 1886. He had a distinguished career that was lost to the vagaries of a divorce action.

Dilke was born at 76 Sloane Street and lived for the rest of his life in this family home. His education was conventional, although he had the advantage of having as tutor at university (Sir) Leslie Stephen – eventual editor of the *Dictionary of National Biography*. He trained as a lawyer, but did not practise, and instead travelled widely, especially within the British Empire, which he regarded always as a beneficial institution. Though radical by temperament he was conservative in lauding the imperialist cause, and in opposing Forster's Education Bill of 1870 because it would diminish the role of the Church in education. However, he was also anti-monarchist at a time when it was unusual to be so, and criticised Queen Victoria for not paying income tax.

He moved within the upper reaches of government but his downfall came unexpectedly when in August 1885 Donald Crawford, MP for Lanark, sued his wife for divorce on the grounds of her adultery with Dilke. This was hotly denied by Dilke, but when the suit was heard in February 1886 Mrs Crawford confessed to adultery and named Dilke. Dilke's advisers persuaded him not to take part in the suit so as to deny the allegation – unwisely as it turns out. Crawford got his decree nisi on the basis of his wife's confession, but before the decree absolute Dilke was able to mount a new court hearing at which he strongly maintained his innocence. Mrs Crawford, however, while admitting adultery with another, unnamed, man, declined to exonerate Dilke. So, Crawford got his divorce and Dilke had to withdraw from public life, especially as he was defeated in the 1886 election anyway.

Though less in the forefront of public affairs, he did return to parliament in 1892, when he was elected by the Forest of Dean constituency.

The Doggett Coat and Badge Race

This venerable and taxing boat race is rowed each 1 August. Its original course was from the Old Swan at London Bridge to the Old Swan at Chelsea, but nowadays from the Swan Steps at London Bridge to the Cadogan Pier east of the Albert Bridge, a distance of about 4¹/₂ miles.

The race derived from the will of Thomas Doggett (1650-1721), an actor comedian, later the manager of Drury Lane Theatre, who left sufficient money 'for procuring yearly on the first day of August for ever, the following particulars, that is to say five pounds for a Badge of Silver weighing about twelve ounces and representing Liberty to be given to be rowed by six young Watermen according to my custom eighteen shillings for Cloath for a livery, whereon the said badge is to be put, one pound one shilling for making up the said Livery and Buttons and appurtances to it and Thirty shillings to the clerk of the Watermens Hall. All which I would have to be continued for ever yearly in commemoration of his Majesty King George's happy accession to the British Throne.'

The orange coat (the colour of the Whig faction in Parliament, whom Doggett favoured), emblazoned with a white Hanoverian horse, has since been replaced by a red coat and an inscribed arm band.

Doggett was manager at Drury Lane when an attempt was made there on the life of George I, and this race possibly was a way of showing his loyalty.

This celebration of the Hanoverian succession is still held under the supervision of the Fishmongers' Company and is the oldest sporting event in the country.

Previously heavy skiffs were used but today light sculling boats are raced against the ebb tide. The usual race time is about 30 minutes.

Dr Dominiceti

In 1765 no. 6 Cheyne Walk was taken by a Venetian doctor with innovative ideas. Bartholomew Dominiceti introduced his 'patent' medicated steam baths for the treatment of anything from asthma to leprosy. One suspects he was prone to exaggeration in other ways, for he claimed to have spent £37,000 – a prodigious sum – on these premises, installing thirty 'sweating chambers' in the garden and four 'fumigating bed

67. *Rowlandson's depiction of the finish at the Swan Inn at Chelsea of the Doggett Coat and Badge race.*

68. *Bartholomew de Dominiceti*

69. *Don Saltero's in Cheyne Walk in 1840.*

chambers'. His patients included the Duke of York and Sir John Fielding, but Dr Johnson declined. However, a letter written by, one, John Dove in 1766, claims that:

> 'I have seen many brought into his house, some leperous, some scrophulous, others hydropical, asthmatical, hectical, ulcerous, rheumatic, flatulent, restless, scorbutic, cancerous etc, all of whom went off cured or greatly relieved; the lame and the blind I have known restored to health and sight.'

Despite such recommendations, Dominiceti seems to have left Cheyne Walk in 1782, hopelessly in debt.

Don Saltero's

The famed coffee house of 'Don Saltero' was at 18 Cheyne Walk. John Salter, once a servant to Sir Hans Sloane and, like his former employer, addicted to collecting curiosities, ran three coffee houses near the Thames at Chelsea before settling for Cheyne Walk. His first venture, probably on the corner with Lawrence Street, was in 1675 when coffee-houses were beginning to be the rage in central London. His famed establishment in Cheyne Walk opened about 1718, but by then his collection of odd items was already a tourist attraction. The *Survey of London* notes that:

> 'His tavern was frequented by all the *literati* of the day, and his Chelsea friends found a warm place. His reputation as a mixer of punch was very high; he could also shave, bleed, draw teeth, and play a little on the fiddle, and every year he added stranger oddities to his queer mimic museum, from which he probably got as much amusement as his many visitors. People vied with one another in presenting strange curios with the most impossible inscriptions to please their host who had not scrupled to advertise himself as a "gimcrack whim collector".'

Salter died in 1728 and was buried in Chelsea. After his death the museum and coffee-house were carried on by his daughter and son-in-law until 1758. In 1799 the collection was sold for only £50 and the coffee-house was turned into a tavern plain and simple. The house became a private residence in 1867.

Duke of York Square

This new development opened in April 2003. Designed by Paul Davis and Partners for the Cadogan estate, it is a mixture of retail outlets and apartments spread over the grounds of the former Royal Military Asylum (*qv*). Immediately prior to the scheme, the premises had been used as a Territorial Army Headquarters.

Grudging approval has come from the architectural press, but the *Guardian* thought the architecture unambitious even though it fitted easily into the local scene, and compared it favourably with Paternoster Square. A second phase, due to open by 2005, will include a new home for the Garden House school, a clinic and more flats and shops including one inside the chapel.

Thomas Faulkner

The first historian to record the history of Chelsea was John Bowack. His *Antiquities of Middlesex* (1705) dealt with the conventional aspects of a number of west London parishes including Chelsea. But the first major historian of Chelsea was a long-time resident, Thomas Faulkner (1777-1855). He published in 1810 *An Historical and Topographical Description of Chelsea and its Environs*, and went on to write books on Fulham, Hammersmith, Kensington and Brentford, Chiswick and Ealing. He reverted to Chelsea in 1829 when a revised 2-volume edition of his first book was published, at first in seventeen monthly parts at 2/6d each.

Faulkner lived at what was then 1 Paradise Row, the site of the later Chelsea Pensioners pub. Here he kept a bookshop and print shop and also described on his business card that

70. Thomas Faulkner, Chelsea historian and bookseller.

he was a 'Teacher of the French, Italian and Spanish Languages. He was also a frequent contributor to the *Gentleman's Magazine*. Earlier works included histories of the Royal Hospital *(qv)* and the Royal Military Asylum *(qv)*.

After Paradise Row he moved to 27 Smith Street where his bookshop, renamed the Cadogan Library, advertised 'an extensive and valuable collection of works in history, divinity, topography, antiquities, voyages and travels, lives and memoirs, poetry and drama'.

A later historian, while acknowledging the public's debt to Faulkner, warns that he did commit many errors in his work on Chelsea, including erroneous copies of inscriptions in Chelsea Old Church.

The Feathers

One of the oldest inns in Chelsea – it is noted in 1664 – stood at the eastern corner of the junction of Cheyne Row and Cheyne Walk. The site is now taken by

71. The riverside scene at Chelsea in 1738. The ferry, loaded with coach and horses, is leaving the Danvers Street landing place.

72. *An extract from the Kip view of Beaufort House 1699 (ill. 14), showing the ferry to the right.*

no. 49 Cheyne Walk. It had extensive gardens to the rear extending nearly to Glebe Place. At a time of coin shortage in 1666, the landlord, Thomas Munday, issued his own halfpenny token.

The Ferry

The horse ferry at Chelsea is possibly referred to in a manuscript of 1292/3 noting the expense for a 'passage of the Thames at Cenlee'. It is mentioned by Norden in 1592 when he included Chelsea in a list of horse ferries over the Thames, and it is seen in a view by Kip of 1699 *(ill. 72)* and by Preist in 1738 *(ill. 71)*, in the latter with a carriage and four on board. In neither of these two prints is an attached horse to be seen, though men may be discerned using oars, so it may be deduced that the services of a horse had by then been dispensed with. On the other hand, a letter, probably sent by Francis Atterbury *(qv)* in 1715, refers to a meeting in Chelsea amongst Jacobite supporters 'by the Horse Ferry at Chelsea'. Atterbury was living in Danvers Street at the time, which is where the ferry docked.

The ferry appears to have been a royal possession, since it was granted in 1618 to a relative of James I, the Earl of Lincoln. The last owner was the Earl Spencer, who held a great deal of land on the opposite bank in Battersea. It was Spencer who spearheaded the campaign to build the first Battersea Bridge which, when constructed and fully opened in 1772, made the ferry a thing of the past.

Flood Street

The name Flood Street was substituted for a bewildering array of individual terraces in 1865. Luke Thomas Flood, who had died five years earlier, had been treasurer of the Chelsea charity schools and a public benefactor. A service, dedicated to his memory, is still held at St Luke's church.

Residents have included the writer Quentin Crew (at no. 33 by 1960), Margaret Thatcher (at No.

73. *Flood Street in 1905.*

53

19). In 1991 when Mrs Thatcher and her husband were thinking of moving elsewhere in Chelsea, it was reported that they had turned down the chance of buying 35 Tite Street, built by Lord Glenconner in 1965, on sale for a mere £7.5 million. Another resident of Flood Street, it is claimed, was William Joyce, the notorious Nazi propagandist in the last war, nicknamed Lord Haw-Haw.

Gorges House

In Kip's view of Beaufort House (*see ill. 14*), a smaller but substantial house is shown to its south-west. This is the gabled Gorges House, built *c*.1600 for Sir Arthur Gorges and his wife, Elizabeth. She was the daughter of the Earl of Lincoln, who briefly occupied the grand mansion of Sir Thomas More, which later became Beaufort House. Gorges, through his wife, later inherited the main property on the death of his father-in-law. One of the earliest entries in the parish registers of Chelsea is the burial of Ambrosia, the 12-year-old daughter of the Gorges.

Gorges House was sold *c*.1664 to a schoolmaster called Josias Priest. In the *London Gazette* of 25 November 1680 appeared the following notice:

> 'Josias Priest, Dancing Master, who kept a Boarding-School of Gentlewomen in Leicester-fields, is removed to the great School-House at Chelsey, that was Mr Portman's. There will continue the same Masters, and others, to the improvement of the said School.'

In this house was given the first performance of Purcell's *Dido and Aeneas*. The libretto bore the words 'An opera performed at Mr Josias Priest's

74. Gough House, from a drawing by M J Rush. The house became the Victoria Hospital for Children.

Boarding School at Chelsey by young gentlewomen.'

Priest, though continuing to live in Chelsea until 1734, appears to have sold the house to Sir William Milman before 1697. Milman's monument was placed in the More Chapel (which he owned) in 1714.

A number of cottages called Milman's Row were built across the site of Gorges House in 1726. These in turn were replaced by borough council housing in 1952.

Gough House

Gough House, which lies between the Physic Garden and the grounds of the Royal Hospital, was built in 1707 for John Vaughan, the Earl of Carbery, whom Pepys describes as 'one of the lewdest fellows of the age'.

Carbery's ownership was succeeded by that of the Gough family, whose fortune was based on trade with India and China. A Mrs Thomas Pemberton began a ladies' school here *c*.1816

Gough House still survives, though nowadays much hemmed in and with its gardens much diminished. In 1866 it was converted to the Victoria Hospital for Children (*qv*). However, the destruction of its interior inevitably then commenced.

A second separate block of the hospital was built, the river embankment of the 1870s took a slice off its garden, and the building of Tite Street, also in the 1870s, took away much more of its grounds. The old building and its more modern wing are now apartments.

75. *Walter Greaves photographed by the statue of Thomas Carlyle (see overleaf).*

76. *The Greaves boatyard in front of Lindsey House in Cheyne Walk. Photograph by James Hedderley.*

Walter and Henry Greaves

The painters, Walter and Henry Greaves, are significant in the history of Chelsea in that they painted either jointly or singly Chelsea scenes before the Embankment was built. In this respect, they were as important as the photographer, James Hedderley (*qv*).

Of the two brothers, Walter was the more proficient. They were sons of a Chelsea waterman and boat operator whose boatyard may be seen above. Walter was born in Lindsey Row, now part of Cheyne Walk, in 1846. When he was 17 the painter James McNeill Whistler came to live a few doors away and so began a lifelong relationship. The two

brothers ferried Whistler about the river just as their father before them had taken J M W Turner to vantage points so that he could paint river scenes. The Greaves brothers helped in Whistler's studio and took art lessons from him. They were, as Whistler once said, his first pupils.

Walter's earlier paintings are full of precision, but gradually under Whistler's influence details became tonal objects and his style was less explicit. He appears to have made very little money from his painting and gave many away even after he was 'discovered' in 1911, rather late in life, by the Goupil Gallery. So impoverished was he in his later years that friends and fellow artists raised a subscription so that he might be housed

in the Charterhouse almshouses in 1922. He died in 1930.

Joyce Grenfell

That marvellous revue artist and raconteur, Joyce Grenfell (1910-79), lived at a number of Chelsea addresses. She was the niece of Nancy Astor, and the daughter of an architect. Though stage-struck while young she gave up any ambition to act when she met and married Reginald Grenfell, an accountant, at the age of 19. Her later career began quite by chance when, at a dinner party in 1939, she was persuaded to recount a talk at a Women's Institute on the subject of 'Useful and Acceptable Gifts'. This so amused and impressed another diner, Herbert Farjeon, that he asked her to appear in a revue he was about to produce

77. *Radclyffe Hall. Photograph by Howard Coster.*

78. *The Pavilion, Henry Holland's house (see overleaf).*

in the West End. Grenfell was an immediate success and her material, manner and genuine personality continued to amuse and fascinate audiences until her retirement. She also appeared in a number of successful films, such as *Genevieve* and *The Yellow Rolls Royce* and was perfect as the bemused games' mistress in the St Trinian films. In 1954 she toured her own one-woman show.

Her pre-marriage days with her family were at 28 St Leonards Terrace, and after marrying she was at no 21 in the same road. From 1939-46 she was at 149 King's Road, moved to no. 114 in 1946 and by 1952 was at no. 149. From 1956 until her death she was at 34 Elm Park Gardens.

Radclyffe Hall

The writer, Marguerite Radclyffe Hall (1880-1943), is best known for her book, *The Well of Loneliness*, which explored the pleasures of lesbianism. This was published by Cape in 1928 and attracted a storm of hysterical outrage. James Douglas, editor of the *Sunday Express* declared in a front-page article,

that 'I would rather give a healthy boy or a healthy girl a phial of prussic acid than this novel. Poison kills the body, but moral poison kills the soul.' The Home Secretary banned the book, whereupon Cape sent the type-moulds to France where it was published and widely distributed by the Pegasus Press. It was as much in demand then as, in more recent years, was *Lady Chatterley's Lover*. Leonard Hill's bookshop in Great Russell Street, the London distributors for Pegasus, was raided by police and copies seized. A court case ensued in which the defence witnesses, E M Forster, Virginia Woolf and Laurence Housman, were not called by the magistrate; he judged the book an 'obscene libel' and ordered the destruction of the copies. Of course, the book became a best-seller and about a million copies were sold during Hall's lifetime.

Radclyffe Hall, who always called herself John, was born into a troubled family but was

able to carve out a life of her own with the aid of a substantial inheritance. She first lived in Chelsea in 1909 when she was at 7 Shelley Court in Tite Street, moved on to 39 Cadogan Square in 1911, and then in 1916 to 1 Swan Walk. In the same year she was at 22 Cadogan Court, Draycott Avenue, her last Chelsea residence, for in 1920 she set up home with Una Troubridge in Brompton.

Hans Town

Richard Horwood's map at the beginning of the 19th century *(ill. 80)* shows Hans Town in its earlier form west and east of Sloane Street. On the west, the rectangle of Hans Place, with its curved ends, is built, and so are a number of side roads. East of Sloane Street is Cadogan Place – through its rear windows could still be seen the river Westbourne snaking its way north to Knightsbridge by today's Harvey Nichols. Beyond the river were fields all the way

79. *Henry Holland, architect and developer.*

nearly to the site of Victoria Station.

The scheme for Hans Town began in 1771 when the distinguished architect, Henry Holland, leased 89 acres from Lord Cadogan for a development which would be named after Sir Hans Sloane, Cadogan's father-in-law. Hans Place was the first to be built, modelled on the Place Vendôme in Paris. To the south of this Holland erected for himself a large house, nicknamed The Pavilion (from his involvement in building the Brighton Pavilion for the Prince Regent). This may be seen in illustrations 78 and 80. To the south of this there were spacious grounds complete with lake, grottoes and a ruined castle folly, landscaped by his father-in-law, 'Capability' Brown.

Jane Austen stayed at no. 23 Hans Place with her brother in 1814-15. Writing to her sister she remarked 'It is a delightful Place, and the garden is quite a Love. I am in the Attic which is the Bedchamber to be preferred.' Her visit was eventful, for she was invited to Carlton House to meet the Prince Regent, who gave her permission to dedicate her novel *Emma* to him.

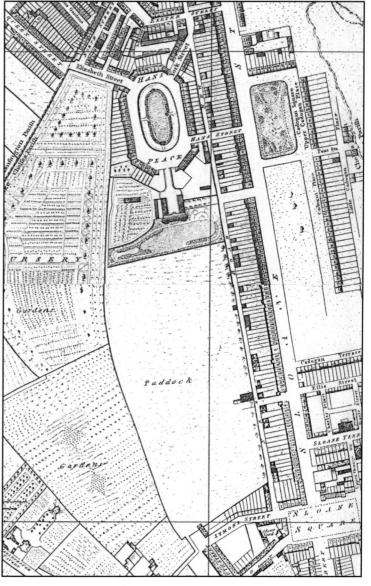

80. *Hans Place and Sloane Street area, from Richard Horwood's map early in the 19th century.*

Other famous names associated with Hans Place are the writer, Laetitia Landon (1802-38) who was born at no. 25 and left when she was 18; the writer Mary Russell Mitford (1787-1855) went to school at no. 22 and lived at no. 33. At the same school run by M. Saint Quentin, Fanny Kemble and Lady Caroline Lamb were pupils. Shelley and Mary Wollstonecraft were at no. 41 in 1817.

Two roads, north-east and south-west of today's Harrod's, were cut through in the 1770s and 1780s to provide access to Hans Town from the Brompton Road. These, now named Hans Crescent and Hans Road, were

changed abruptly as the heart of the village, once down by the riverside, shifted inexorably northwards to the King's Road. Many of his pictures are reproduced in *Chelsea seen from its early days*, by John Bignell *(qv)*, himself a noted photographer of the area at a time before substantial changes were made in modern times.

Henry VIII

King Henry VIII (1491-1547) had a significant impact on early Chelsea history. It was he that allowed the execution of Sir Thomas More *(qv)*, whose house (later called Beaufort House *qv*) dominated the Chelsea riverside. Henry visited More, his Lord Chancellor after the disposal of Wolsey, at Chelsea several times, travelling up river from Westminster. During their good times they discussed, according to More's son-in-law William Roper, 'matters of astronomy, geometry, divinity and wordly affairs'.

However, by 1530 Henry, bereft of a male heir, was anxious to secure a divorce from

81. A James Hedderley photograph of Lombard Street and Arch House, looking east, before the building of the Embankment in the 1870s. Lombard Street and its continuation, Duke Street, ran between Old Church Street and Beaufort Street, parallel to the river.

82. King Henry VIII, after Hans Holbein.

small houses which deteriorated very quickly in social status. Both lost one of their sides to the expansion of Harrod's.

The Hans Town scheme did not withstand the pressures of late 19th-century developers catering for well-to-do customers. The modest and moderately-priced houses of Hans Place were demolished in favour of grander houses, but the most significant loss was The Pavilion over whose site and generous grounds Cadogan Square *(qv)* was built.

James Hedderley

Hedderley photographed Chelsea before the Embankment was built, his pictures benefiting from the clarity that came from large long-exposure cameras. He was born in 1815, and for a time was a sign writer in Duke Street, a short road parallel to the Thames between Old Church Street and Beaufort Street. He then moved to Riley Street at World's End, itself an area to see much demolition as Cheyne Walk was embanked. Hedderley's Chelsea was

Catherine of Aragon and More, unable to agree with this, resigned from the Lord Chancellorship and retired to Chelsea. For refusing to accept the king's claim that he, rather than the Pope, was head of the Church in England, More was executed in 1535.

Then, with the lack of a guilty conscience for which he was renowned, Henry acquired Chelsea manor within months of More's death and built a new manor house virtually next door to More's old property. It was Henry's house that was later lived in by Sir Hans Sloane.

Holy Trinity

Holy Trinity in Sloane Street, consecrated in 1890, is one of the most spectacular churches in London. It was designed by John Dando Sedding, though much of the arts and crafts embellishment, which gives the church its reputation, was added by Henry Wilson and Ernest Gimson after Sedding's death in 1891. The large east window was designed by Edward Burne-Jones and made under the supervision of William Morris.

The building is on the site of a previous Holy Trinity, built to cater for the population which had moved into Hans Town. Consecrated in 1830, its first vicar was a former curate from St Luke's, the Rev. H Blunt.

The earlier church was designed by James Savage, who had built the distinguished St Luke's Chelsea, but the building was not highly regarded. The Chelsea historian, Alfred Beaver, described it as 'a melange of Gothic items of various periods' and said that it was much criticised even at the time of its erection. In the event, this chapel-of-ease to St Luke's was too small for the vastly growing popula-

83. Holy Trinity Church, Sloane Street.

tion of the area and was demolished to make way for Sedding's building.

Leigh Hunt

The journalist and poet, Leigh Hunt (1784-1859), is a largely forgotten writer nowadays, but he was highly regarded and notorious in his time. As a schoolboy he was timid and bullied, but he made friends with Thomas Barnes, later to be editor of *The Times*, and he himself developed a flair for journalism in the radical tradition. Together with his brother he published a paper called *The Examiner*, which strongly advocated reform of Parliament. Three times the government prosecuted them for their publications but on no occasion was it successful.

However, in 1812, when re-publican feelings were running high, they were prosecuted for libelling the Prince Regent. Hunt was merely reacting to a particularly unctuous description of the Prince in another paper by repeating its words and adding some of his own:

'This Adonis in loveliness was a corpulent man of fifty! – this delightful, blissful, wise, honourable, virtuous, true and immortal prince was a violator of his word, a libertine over head and ears in disgrace, a despiser of domestic ties, the companion of gamblers and demireps, a man who has just closed half a century without one single claim on the gratitude of his country or the respect of posterity'.

For this the brothers were sentenced in 1813 to two years

84. Leigh Hunt.

85. Holman Hunt's house in Cheyne Walk, at the corner with Lawrence Street. From a drawing by Walter Greaves.

in gaol. Hunt, incarcerated at Clerkenwell, had a trellis with flowers built in his cell; the ceiling was painted with sky and clouds, and Venetian blinds were put up at the window. Many visitors came to see him and he was on intimate terms with Byron, Shelley and Keats. Indeed it was Hunt who in 1816 championed the talents of the latter two poets to the nation. Hunt, his wife and seven children sailed to Italy in 1821 to see Shelley and Byron and was present when Shelley's body was cremated there in 1822, and it was Hunt who wrote the epitaph on his tomb.

Hunt's connection with Chelsea began in 1833 when he moved into 22 Upper Cheyne Row. He was instrumental in finding a house for his friend, Thomas Carlyle, in Cheyne Row the following year. Hunt later moved to Hammersmith, impoverished by a large family and a wife who had taken to drink. Many friends came to his rescue – Dickens gave readings for him, the government granted him £200, and he obtained, surprisingly in the circumstances, a royal grant of £200. He is buried in Kensal Green cemetery, his grave marked by a sadly depleted monument.

William Holman Hunt

The painter William Holman Hunt (1827-1910) lived from 1850 to 1853 at 59 Cheyne Walk, a house demolished eventually when the Cheyne Hospital for Children was rebuilt. Here he painted the first version of The Light of the World (1854). Two years earlier his Chelsea neighbour, Thomas Carlyle, had declared Hunt's The Hireling Shepherd as 'the greatest picture he had seen painted by any modern man'.

The Dictionary of National Biography credits Hunt and Ford Madox Brown as the founders of the Pre-Raphaelite movement, though Dante Rossetti became its most famous advocate. From 1878 Hunt had a studio in Manresa Road where he painted one of his most famous works, The Triumph of the Innocents. Hunt also unveiled the bust of Dante Rossetti on the Embankment gardens; it was sculpted by Ford Madox Brown.

Augustus John

The painter Augustus John (1878-1961) was 'Chelsea artist' writ large. With a commanding presence, a red beard, a broad artist's hat and a cloak, there was no mistaking his figure, Bohemian in a Bohemian era. Born in Tenby, Wales, he studied art at the Slade School, with his sister Gwen, and was very highly regarded there. In 1897

86. *Self portrait of Augustus John, c.1901.*

King's Head and Eight Bells

One of the oldest and most famous of Chelsea's pubs is now a restaurant called La Chaumiere. Situated at the western corner of Cheyne Row and Cheyne Walk, it was one of the numerous public houses lining the riverside before the Embankment was constructed. It survived that upheaval but has fallen foul in the last year or two to the economics of public houses.

In 1871 it boasted that it had been in existence for over a hundred years, though this probably understated its age. The present building dates from 1886. There are, according to local historian Tom Pocock, cellars thought to be Tudor. During the first half of the 20th century it was a venue for many Chelsea artists. It seemed in the post-war years, says Pocock, 'the ultimate Chelsea pub with bearded artists, boozy writers (Dylan Thomas was a regular), Chelsea pensioners and the pub's darts team practising in the public bar (with sawdust on the floor).'

In the 1960s came disaster. Again according to Tom Pocock, the pub's owners, Whitbread, ordered the stripping of the interior – the mahogany and the mirrors, and in their place put high stools along with an 'American bar', a plastic vine, wrought-iron table lamps with pink shades, foam-backed carpet and a tank of tropical fish.

Whitbread soon learned that they had made a mistake and back came Victoriana – but fake – and some of the old clientele returned as well, attracted by better cuisine. But it was not to last. Under succeeding landlords the pub did not prosper and in 2002 it was put up for sale.

he hit his head while diving into the sea in Wales and from that time his personality changed, so that he became more dramatic in his ways and manner.

In 1914, after years spent in the Fitzrovia artists' scene, he moved to Chelsea where he had Robert van Hoff build a house for him at 28 Mallord Street, as a copy of Rembrandt's studio house in Amsterdam. (It was later occupied by another ebullient figure, the entertainer Gracie Fields.) By then John was probably the best known living painter in England, renowned for his portraits, which included those of George Bernard Shaw and David Lloyd George. In 1935 he moved to 49 Glebe Place and in 1940 to 33 Tite Street where he still resided off and on in 1958.

Kensal New Town

Built between two railway lines, the old LNWR and the Great Western, in north Kensington, and bisected by the Grand Junction Canal and the Harrow Road is Kensal New Town and Queens Park. Oddly, this area once belonged to Chelsea, a result of a manorial grant in medieval times, which was perpetuated until the reorganisation of London boroughs in 1899. The area, by then very down-at-heel, and a drain on the rates, was assigned to Kensington who did not want it at all.

It consisted of about 140 acres and was merely rural land until the coming of the canal, the railways and the Western Gas Works. In addition, Kensal Green cemetery to the west provided employment.

87. *The King's Head and Eight Bells, Cheyne Walk, in 1858, by Walter and Henry Greaves.*

The King's Road

Chelsea's high street was still very much a rural road in the early 19th century, with fields and nursery gardens on both sides. It was not, as it is today, the hub of Chelsea, for that was still down by the river around the Old Church. Indeed, the eastern stretch of King's Road was, as its name implies, the King's Private Road, from the east side of Sloane Square (where it crossed the river Westbourne via the Bloody Bridge) to Old Church Street, and did not become officially a public road until 1830. It was used by Charles II on his way to Hampton Court, and by George III visiting his palace at Kew. This difficulty of access (by token only) necessarily had an effect on development in the road itself, though roads north and south of it had already sprung up.

William Rothenstein (1872-1945), a friend of Whistler and Wilde, said of the King's Road that 'It is shabbier than Oxford Street, with its straggling dirty, stucco mid-century houses and shops.' Many of those buildings survive and he would no doubt be surprised that they are pursued so advidly by retailers.

King's Road has suffered some awful blemishes – notably a supermarket and a disastrously ugly fire station, but its main problems today are the control of traffic, the explosion of food outlets and the abundance of visitors. Since the 1960s, retailing of clothes has also become serious business here.

It may be argued that modern clothes retailing began with Mary Quant, who set up her first shop in the later 1950s at the bow-fronted Markham House in the King's Road, next to Markham Square. It was just a few steps from the then dowdy Markham pub which enjoyed an unexpected rejuvenation as the shop became fashionable. (The pub now houses a building society and coffee house.)

The pace has been frenetic ever since. While Carnaby Street in the West End catered for the tourist, so the King's Road set its sights on customers in search of better-made fashion. At the same time bars, restaurants and antique shops proliferated, undaunted by the rise in rents. It is difficult now to imagine what trades, what attractions, previously occupied these shops after the last war. The directory page reproduced as illustration 88, takes us back even further to an even less sophisticated era of retailing.

56 & 400 *Home & Colonial Stores Ltd*
58 Wagstaff Herbert Henry, hosier
60 to 70 Traylen Frank Whitwell, fancy draper
.. *here is Blacklands terrace* ..
72 *Colville tavern*, Pioneer Catering Co. Ltd
.... *here is Lincoln street* ....
74 Legg Chas.Sidney,ladies' outfittr
76 Goodman Bros. stationers
78 Blake Mrs. Charlotte, greengro
80 Rees William, fancy draper
82 Staple John, artificial teeth mfr
82 Passmore J. & Son, chemists
84 Smith Alfred John & Co.Limited, wine merchants
84 Goodbody Alfred George, artificial teeth manufacturer
86 Salmon & Gluckstein Limited, tobacconists
88 Nash George Mark, baker
90 Andrews & Co. butchers
92, 94 & 96 *Boots Cash Chemists (Southern) Ltd*
98 Lipton Limited, tea merchants
100 Fowler Alfred William, hosier
102to106 Wakeford Bros. liz.endrprs
108OsbornHarry,baby linen wareho
.... *here is Anderson street* ....
110 Leverett & Frye Lim. grocers
112 Parker Arthur, fancy draper
114 O'Dell Miss Grace,court dressma
114 Fleming, Reid & Co.Ltd.hosiers
116A, Mulvey Wm. John. vet. surgn
116B, & 305 Hammond Mrs. Kate, florist
116C, Ayliffe Wm. & Sons,bootmas
.... *here is Tryon street* .....
118 Bloomberg Hyman &Son,tailrs
120 Crapper Thomas & Co. Ltd. sanitary engineers
122 Glover George & Co. Ltd. dry gas meter makers
122A, Smyth Randolph Marriott, surveyor of taxes
122A, Collins William, customs & excise officer
122A, Colley Edward John, customs & excise officer
124 & 124A, Webb, Sons & Clarke Ltd. wholesale cheesemongers
126 Fryer Mrs. Ellen, confectioner
126 Reeves Gilbert & Co. wine & spirit merchants
128 & 185,353 & 355 Harding Fredk & Sons, boot & shoe makers
130 Genini Samuel, dining rooms
132 Bleek Charles, fishmonger
.... *here is Bywater street* ....
134 Beaton George Alex. baker
136 Williams Frank, tobacconist
138 *Markham Arms*, Harry Arthur Andrews
138A, Wilkins George Frederick, LL.B. solicitor
.. *here is Markham square* ..
140 *London&South WesternBank Ld.* O. H. Marsh, manager
144 & 198 Williams Daniel & Co. linendrapers
146 Dupont Mrs. Emily, tailor
.... *here is Markham street* ....
148 & 150 *Imperial Playhouses*, Chambers & Smurthwaite,proprs
152 JoubertAmédée&Son,upholstrs
152 Nicholson William, artist
154 Hudson Edmund, physician & surgeon
154 Seward George Halifax, surgeon dentist
156 Madderton & Co. Ltd. artists' colormen
158 Hiscock John Henry, oilman
160 Gigner John & Co. chemists
162 Bloomberg Mark, tailor
.. *here is Jubilee place* ..
164 RADNOR MANSION:—
2 Digby Miss
3 Olive Miss

166 Kohl Mrs. Alice, tea rooms
168 TreadwellBros. boot & shoe ma
170 Robinson William & Co. dyers
172 Orsborn John Harry, butcher
174 *Singer Sewing Machine Co.* Ld
176 Hedley MadameMarthe, millnr
176B, King Henry, bootmaker
... *here is Blenheim street* ....

184 Ashby George & Sons, electric light engineers
184 Nicholl Bros. laundry
181 Collins Thomas, boot & shoe ma
186 Miller Arthur. furniture dealer
188 Howells David, wardrobe dlr
190 & 466 Duerre Arthur George & Sons, watchmakers
192 Bull Arthur & Co. hosiers
194 Defrae Joseph, hairdresser
196 & 506 Brazil Walter, pork btchr
198 & 144 Williams Daniel & Co. linendrapers
200 *Lord Nelson*,Wm. Jas. Stephens
202 WhiteMrs.Gertrude,tobacconst
204 Cocks R. M.& Son,estate agents
206 Robinson William Edward,M.D. physician & surgeon
208 Gordon Albert. photographer
212 Steel Thomas & Sons, carpntrs
214 Crosby Alfred Edward Binnington, dentist
216 Cole James, watchmaker
218 Archer George, fried fish dealer
220 Oliver Douglas, cycle maker
222 Myers Henry, tobacconist
222A, Lucas Mrs. Olive, servants' registry office
.. *here is Upper Manor street* ..
224 *London County & Westminster Bank Ltd.* Austin Hardwicke Neame, manager
226A, Buck Miss Rose
232 POSTAL Telegraph Office, Receiving House,MoneyOrder Office & Savings Bank
Chelsea Palace (music hall)
.... *here is Sydney street* ....
250 *Chelsea (Offices of Clerk to the Guardians of)*, Charles W. Shepherd, clerk & supt.registr
.. *here are Arthur street & St. Luke's burial ground* ..
262 Beazley George, plumber
264 Cranford Mrs. Sarah, antique furniture dealer
266 Pidgeon Miss Ellen,refrshmt. rms
276 Adams Bernard Robert, artist
276 French Miss Isabel M. artist
278 Randell Thomas, mail cart ma
.... *here is Manresa road* ....
280 Robinson T. J. & Son, solicitors
282 Bevan Henry, house agent
292 March&Co.antique furntre.dlrs
292 Gloag Miss Isabell L. artist
294 Holton Mrs. Elizh. serv. reg. off
Chelsea Pleasant Saturday Evening Approved Society, Richard V. Holton, sec

296 CARLYLE STUDIOS:—
1 McMullin John
1A, Rowe Algernon, artist
2 Carter William, artist
4 Parkes Miss Uellina, artist
6 Sutton Mrs
.... *here is Carlyle square* ....
298 *Cadogan Arms*, WilliamKnight
.... *here is Church street* ....
300 Parr's Bank Ltd.
Ernest Hy. Youngman, man
VALE TERRACE:—
1 Weigall Gerald
2 Radcliffe-Smith Miss
3 Symes Arthur William
6 Hinkley Ernest Edwd.fruitr
7 LaffeatyThos.Jno.cycle ma
8A, Bingham Brig.-Gen. Hon. Francis Richard, C.B
9 Lindsay Miss
10 Pearce Frank, artists' clrmn
10A, Bogle Stewart
12DerbyMissHelenB.restaurnt
12A, Jackson Miss
.... *here is Vale avenue* ....
338 Billings Wm. Charles & Sons Ltd. corn dealers
340 Jones Timothy, dairyman
344 & 346 *Beaufort Drapery Co*
.... *here is Beaufort street* ....
348 & 350 *Roebuck*, Mrs. Amy Clarke
356 Gillett Mrs. Eliza, eel pie house
362 & 436 Nurse Arthur Albert & Co. greengrocers
366 Courts Bernard, clothier
370 Wilmshurst Joseph, plumber
370 Goldstein Jacob, tailor
372 Payn Arthur John, saddler
374 Stebbing Saml. Jas. butcher
376 & 378 Allen Thomas, hatter
here are Chelsea Park dwellings
380 Vedy Alfred Fredk. newsagent

KING'S HOUSE STUDIOS:—
1 Houghton William, artist
2 Butler Frank Edwd. artist
3 Pitcher N. Sotheby, artist
4 Greenwood Sidney Earnshaw, artist

394 *Chelsea, South Kensington & Fulham Permanent Building Society*, Frodk. Davison, sec
396 White George, printer
400&56 *Home & Colonial Stores Ltd*
402 Chorley James Ltd. grocers
404 Brodie Miss Ivy, milliner
405 Jordan Wm.&Thos.leathr.mers
403 Dawkins Alfred, seed merchnt
425 *Stanley Ward Conservative Club*, George P. Hall, sec
430 Thorn Joseph. pawnbroker
432 Timmis & Richards, chemists
434 Richards Thomas William, paperhangings dealer
436 & 362 Nurse Arthur Albert & Co. greengrocers
438 Hunt Wright Albt. linendraper
440&277 Lambert James Frederick, furniture dealer
.... *here is Limerston street* ....
442*StanleyArms*,Donald Wm.Clark
444 Carter Richard & Sons, builders
446 McKee George
448 *National Society for the Prevention of Cruelty to Children (Incorporated)*, J. Newlove, inspector
452 Hodgson Misses
454 Woollaston Charles, builder
456 Monaghan ThomasJoseph,M.D. physician & surgeon
.... *here is Hobury street* ....
458 Wing Mrs
466 & 190 Duerre Arthur George & Sons, watchmakers
470Hindmarsh Fdk.ball bearings rpr
.... *here is Shalcomb street* ....
476 Strohl Joseph, decorator
478 Hymus Albert, hairdresser
480 Ford Fredk. Isaac, furn.remvr
484 & 439 Dale William, greengrocer
488 Matthise Theodore, baker
490A & 155 & 327 Lond & Western Ltd. laundry
.... *here is Langton road* ....
492 Monk William Henry, grocer
494 Moore Alfred John, dining rms
496 Buckenham Mrs.Louisa, linendraper
498 Frost S. & Co. Ltd. provsn.mers
500 *Wetherby Arms*,JohnLonghurst
.... *here is Slaidburn street* ....
502 Schafer William, baker
504 Evans Edward James, dairy
506 & 196 Brazil Walter, pork btchr
508 Murdoch Misses Mary Ann & Georgina, corn & flour dealrs
Riches Geo. Robt. newsagent
510 { POST, Money Order Office & Savings Bank
512 Norris Frank Walter, wine & spirit merchant
...... *here is Edith grove* ......
514 Cary Joseph, physician & surgn
518 Staples Miss Catherine,dress ma
534 Bender Rev.HermannChas.B.A
.... *here is Fernshaw road* ....
536 Bull William &Sons,nurserymn
..... *here is Gunter grove* .....
538 *Church Sisters' Home*, Miss Jean Peacock, supt
540 Clementson Fredk. Wm. artist
544 *National Window Cleaners(The)*
544 & 546 *National Furniture Depositories (The)*
.... *here is Hortensia road* ....
550 *St. Mark's College (National Society's Training College for Schoolmasters)*, Rev.Robt.Hudson,M.A.prncpl
550 *London (2nd) (City of London) General Hospital, R.A.M.C. (Territorial Force)*, Lt.-Col. Eustace MaudeCallender,M.D. commdg. (St. Mark's college)
[For remainder of names on this side,see King's road,Fulham, in "COUNTY SUBURBS DIRECTORY"]

SOUTH SIDE

15 *Midland Railway Co.'s Booking, Receiving & General Enquiry Office*, By. Jas. Thomas, agt
17 Davis Alfred, printseller
19 & 125 Jesson Ernest,greengrocer
19 Libowitch Simon, ladies' tailor
21 StephensonFrank&Co.fishmngrs
23 Adam James, tailor
25 Williamson Ltd. confectioners
27 Robert Ghislain, chemist
29 Pickett ThomasWilliam Harold, chemist
29A, Delbruck Raoul Ernest, anæsthetist
31 Bishop & Co. tobacconists
31 Moy Benjamin, chiropodist
DUKE OF YORK'S HEADQUARTERS:—
18th (County of London) Battalion (London Irish Rifles), LondonRegiment(Territorial Force), Lt.-Col. E. G. Concanon, D.S.O.,T.D. commdg
London (6th) Field Ambulance, R.A.M.C.(Territorial Force), Lt.-Col. J. Moyle O'Connor, commanding
London (4th) General Hospital, R.A.M.C.(TerritorialForce), Lt.-Col. A. Thorne, M.B. commanding
London (2nd) Sanitary Company,R.A.M.C. (Territorial Force), Major O. Goddard, commanding
County of London (1st) Yeomanry (Middlesex) (Duke of Cambridge's Hussars) (Territorial Force), Lt.-Col. Sir Mathew RichardHy.Wilson, C.S.I., M.P. commanding
King Edward's Horse, Yeomanry (The King's Oversea Dominions Regiment) (Territorial Force) (Special Reserves), Lt.-Col. V. S. Sandeman, commanding
London (2nd) Division (Territorial Force), Maj.-Gen. Morland, general officer commanding
London (2nd) Divisional Royal Engineers(Territorial Force) (Administrative Centre), Capt. E. V. Spencer, commanding
London Mounted Brigade (Territorial Force), Col. A. H. M. Taylor, D.S.O. brigade commander; Capt. C. S. Rome, brigade major
London (2nd) Divisional Artillery (Territorial Force), Col. J. C. Wray, M.V.O. commanding
London (2nd) DivisionalTransport& Supply Column,A.S.C. (Territorial Force), Lt.-Col. O. F. T.Blyth,commanding
London (1st) Field Ambulance, R.A.M.C.(TerritorialForce), Lt.-Col. R. R. Sleman, M.D. commanding
London(2nd) Field Ambulance, R.A.M.C.(TerritorialForce), Lt.-Col. William Salisbury Sharpe, M.D. commanding
London (3rd)Field Ambulance, R.A.M.C.(Territorial Force), Lt.-Col. J. R. Whait, M.B. commanding
London (1st) (City of London) SanitaryCompany,R.A.M.C. (Territorial Force), Major L. T. F. Bryett, M.D. comdg
Royal Engineer Cadets (2nd LondonDivision)(Territorial Force), Lt. F. R. Cullingford, commanding officer
Territorial Force Association of the County of London, Col. J. C. Oughterson, sec
.. *here is Cheltenham terrace* ..
Whitelands College (National Society's Training College for Schoolmistresses in Elementary Schools), Miss C. G. Luard, principal
.... *here is Walpole street* ....
35 & 37 Battersby Wm.pawnbroker
39 Hill Frank, photographer
39 Alden Ernest, carver & gilder
41 Steggall William, butcher

88. *A page from Kelly's Directory for King's Road in 1906, showing the traders then operating.*

89 and 90. The Duke of York Square development, off the King's Road, soon after opening in April 2003.

91. Old-style King's Road shops in 2003.

92. A former Temperance billiard hall in the King's Road now used for selling antiques.

Lawrence Street

Lawrence Street, to the east of the Old Church, is one of the oldest roads in Chelsea. It derives its name from the owner of the earliest known Chelsea Manor House, Sir Thomas Lawrence, a goldsmith. He bought the manor and the house (probably a 16th-century building located at the northern end of today's Lawrence Street) in 1583. He died ten years later and was buried in a medieval chapel in the Old Church, which subsequently became known as the Lawrence Chapel.

It was in the north-western side of Lawrence Street that the Chelsea Porcelain Factory (*qv*) was located. The junction with Justice Walk is its site.

Lawrence Street was once intimately adjacent to the Thames (*see ill. 61*), but after the Embankment was constructed the street and river were physically divided and with the growth of fast traffic even more so.

Henry James used rooms at 10 Lawrence Street in which to write, while he himself lived at his club. However, persuaded by the charm of Chelsea's atmosphere, he moved into 21 Carlyle Mansions in 1913, which he described as his 'Chelsea perch ... the haunt of the sage and seagull'. The creator of *The Beggar's Opera*, John Gay, was at no. 16 in 1712-14, the same address as Tobias Smollett, the writer, in 1750-62. According to the *Dictionary of National Biography*, the cleric David Williams (1738-1816), founder of the Royal Literary Fund, married a wife without a fortune and set up home and a school in Lawrence Street in 1773.

Lindsey House

The substantial Lindsey House, built *c.*1674, possibly on the site of an earlier house, is now numbered 98-100 Cheyne Walk. Its most notable owner was Count Zinzendorf, who established here in 1751 a Moravian religious sect (*qv*), but which lasted as occupiers only until 1770. The house in this period was much altered and about 1775 it was divided into separate dwellings, at which time it lost many of its exterior and interior features as well, of course, having additional front doors inserted into its window bays.

The painter, Whistler, lived at adjacent no. 96 from 1866 to 1878, and made the acquaintance of the nearby Greaves brothers (*qv*).

Less well known is that the great engineers Marc Brunel and his son, Isambard Kingdom Brunel, lived at no. 98 by 1808 until at least 1825. It was in the latter year that Brunel snr began what was to be an extended and hazardous venture – the building of the Thames Tunnel (today part of the London underground system). Isambard eventually completed it.

93. Lindsey House.

Little Chelsea

Little Chelsea defined that area extending from Chelsea Creek (the western boundary with Fulham) and the odd kink in the King's Road that is familiar today. Hamilton's map of 1664 shows it almost empty of houses apart from Stanley House by the creek (the site now occupied by St Mark's College *qv*), but there was also a house in the vicinity used by Sir Francis Kynaston in 1636 for his Museum Minervae. This was a school for sons of noblemen and gentlemen which began in Bedford Street, Covent Garden, *c*.1632. Kynaston a courtier of Charles I, was 'cup-bearer' to the king but, according to a contemporary report, had to resign the position because he trembled so much from nervousness. At his school Latin, Greek, Hebrew, Spanish, French, Italian and German were taught.

Another house was built by Sir James Smith in 1635. This was rebuilt or extensively altered, probably *c*.1700, by Anthony Ashley Cooper, the 3rd Earl of Shaftesbury, a close friend of Joseph Addison, resident of Sands End House on the other side of the creek. Shaftesbury's house was then bought by a collector of books and antiquities rejoicing in the name of Narcissus Luttrell (1657-1732), who left a diary of national events which is sometimes of interest to London historians. In the 19th century the house was converted into a workhouse for the parish of St George's Hanover Square. Its site is now occupied by the Chelsea and Westminster Hospital in the Fulham Road.

Both Chelsea and Kensington vestries had their own wharves – mainly to take on coal, timber and stone – on the stretch of river south-west of Cremorne Road.

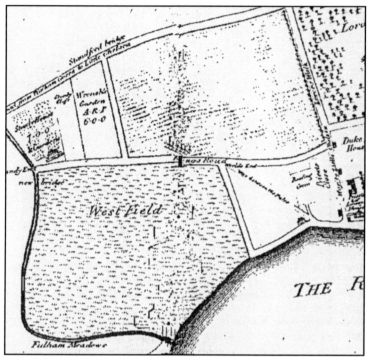

94. *Little Chelsea, to the far west of Chelsea, as shown on Hamilton's map of 1677. Chelsea Creek is to the left.*

Lombard Street

Lombard Street and its extension Duke Street mostly disappeared when Cheyne Walk was embanked in the 1870s. As the sketch map by Barbara Denny below shows, they ran parallel to the Thames, from Old Church Street to Beaufort Street. At its eastern end Lombard Street went beneath Arch House, as illustration 33, by Walter Greaves, shows. He also drew the riverside frontage of Lombard Street, picturing the Adam and Eve with its steps down to the foreshore, and the Old Ferry Wharf where coal was unloaded.

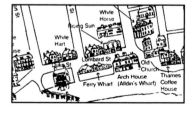

London Sketch Club

This Club, which has its roots in the Langham Sketching Club in Bond Street, has been at 7 Dilke Street for over forty-five years. Its origins may be traced back to the Artists' Society, founded in 1830 and based in a studio in Fitzrovia. In 1838 a sketching section was formed, an activity which grew in importance with the increase of illustrated magazines, newspapers and books. This group became the Langham Sketching Club (meeting at Langham Place in the West End), and in 1898 it was officially formed as the London Sketch Club. In 1957 the Club moved to Dilke Street in Chelsea.

Members have included Phil May, H M Bateman, John Hassall, Christopher Nevinson, Heath Robinson, Baden-Powell and Arthur Conan Doyle.

95. *Lots Road Power Station in the 1920s.*

Lots Road Power Station

The road derives its name from land in the neighbourhood called 'The Lots', about 4 acres of manorial land which could be used by manorial tenants to pasture their animals after Lammas Day (13 August) until sowing time. On the north they were fronted by Ashburnham House (hence Ashburnham Road), built in 1747, but probably on the site of an earlier family house.

It could be a bleak area in poor weather, and the Thames particularly dangerous. Sir William Ashburnham in the 17th century was saved from being lost on the river in fog by the sound of the bell in the Old Church. In gratitude he donated a new bell to the church in 1679, which today is displayed there. In the vicinity in the 19th century Cremorne pleasure gardens (*qv*) entertained thousands of Londoners.

By the beginning of the 20th century the area was quite the opposite of a pleasure ground, full of terraces of houses without bathrooms, with noisome industries fronting a filthy river.

In 1902 the site was acquired by the District Railway, by then owned by transportation entrepreneur, Charles Tyson Yerkes (1837-1905), an American. He was then in the process of building up what is now the inner part of the London underground system. Not only did his company come to own the District and Metropolitan lines, but also the Bakerloo, Central, Piccadilly and Northern. What he needed was a guaranteed power system, independent of the numerous private and local authority companies which provided electricity in London. His acquisition of the Brompton & Piccadilly line included with it a plan to build a small generating station at Lots Road. It was therefore a brave enterprise to

build a power station large enough to satisfy the other lines as well. He probably chose Lots Road for his expanded plan because the site was cheap and, being next to the river, convenient for the importation of coal – on an average day, when the station was fully operational, about 750 tons were used. Also, most importantly, there was an artesian well beneath, which supplied the boilers.

The engineer/architect of this massive building was another American, James Russell Chapman. Work began in 1902 with the sinking of 220 concrete piles as foundation. The building was to be 453 ft long, 175ft wide and 140 ft high to the roof apex. Above that were the four brick chimneys 275ft high – these have dominated west Chelsea ever since. First supplies to the underground began in June 1905 when Yerkes was receiving complaints from Chelsea neighbours about the noise

96. A cartoon in Punch in 1906, relating to an MP's request for more statues on the Embankment. Punch suggested an equestrian statue of Thomas Carlyle mounted on the four chimneys of Lots Road power station.

from the turbines and the pollution from the chimneys. In 1907 Chelsea Council prosecuted the company for the black smoke issuing from the chimneys, alleging that while the company had, by the use of electricity, removed the smoke that used to gather in the steam-driven Metropolitan and District lines, it was now discharging it over the citizens of Battersea and Chelsea instead. The Council lost its case and had to pay costs.

Coal use was abandoned altogether in 1965 and gradually the power for the Underground system was obtained from the National Grid. The end of the power station came on 21 October 2002, when the Transport Minister, John Spellar, switched off the last working turbine.

Two of the four chimneys have been demolished and the building and its environs are subject to planning applications now being pursued by a corporate entity called Circadian.

Magpie and Stump

The Magpie and Stump public house was on the waterfront in Cheyne Walk. It was certainly there in Tudor times, for Henry VIII, then lord of Chelsea manor, granted it a strip of land. At a time when manor courts were important in local governance, it was host to their proceedings. In 1803 conspirators led by Col. Despard, plotting to kill George III and steal the Crown Jewels, met here.

The Pye, as it was usually called, managed to survive the creation of the Embankment but fell victim to a fire in 1886. On part of its site the architect, Charles Robert Ashbee *(qv)*, built a house for his mother, and an office for himself on the old skittle ground, which he called Magpie and Stump. This was no. 37 and he also built nos. 38 and 39 on the rest of the site. He himself lived at no 74 Cheyne Walk, which he also designed, from 1898-1902 – this house was lost to a landmine in 1941. Unfortunately No. 37 was demolished in 1968 to make way for a dreary block of flats, though the other two houses remain.

Hortense Mancini

The life of Hortense Mancini (1647-1699) contained the sort of scandal that neatly suited the Restoration years. She was a niece and heiress of the wealthy Cardinal Mazarin and spent much of her younger days at the French court, where she caught the eye of Charles II, then in exile from England. However, she was married, or rather sold, to a religious fanatic, the Duc de la Meilleraye, who not only obtained her fortune but also renamed himself the Duc de Mazarin. It was an absurd mismatch of a marriage and she escaped as soon as possible, especially as

97. Houses built by C R Ashbee at 38-9 Cheyne Walk on the site of the Magpie and Stump.

her husband had contrived to have her shut in a monastery to escape life's temptations. Legend has it that she travelled, disguised as a boy, across Europe, to reach the sanctuary of London, where she re-established a relationship with Charles II, now on the throne and able to make her an allowance of £4,000. This was a considerable sum, but not enough to sustain a spendthrift and gambler like Hortense and when the king died in 1685 she was in considerable financial difficulty.

She had many scandalous liaisons – 'It was a story all the world knew' said John Evelyn – but because of her reduced circumstances she had to retire to a house in Paradise Row in Chelsea (now Royal Hospital Road) accompanied by an elderly admirer, Sr de St Egremont (or Evremond). Old though he was, she died before him. Her absurd and distant husband claimed her body, which he had embalmed so that it could travel with him on his many journeys in France.

98. Hortense Mancini, from a painting by Pierre Mignard.

99. Dr Richard Mead.

Karl Marx

Marx (1818-83) came to live in Chelsea, together with his wife Jenny and (then) three children in 1849 at a momentous time in Europe. With Engels and others he had published the Communist Manifesto in 1848, in effect a call to arms directed at the working-classes when much of Europe was in a ferment of revolutionary ideas. Marx, born in Trier, Germany, was forced to flee his own country, hence his arrival in England.

His first London home was 4 Anderson Street, Chelsea, just off the King's Road. Here he and his family stayed for about six months before bailiffs evicted them for non-payment of rent. His wife, Jenny recalled:

'We had to leave the house the next day. It was cold, rainy and dull. My husband looked for accommodation for us. When he mentioned the four children, nobody would take us in. Finally a friend helped us, we paid our rent and I hastily sold all my beds to pay the chemist, the baker, the butcher and the milkman who, alarmed at the sight of the sequestration, suddenly besieged me with their bills.'

They moved on to the German Hotel in Leicester Square (now Manzi's restaurant) and were thrown out of there also for not paying their rent. Then they moved to Dean Street for 5 years – the restaurant Quo Vadis bears a plaque to that effect.

Dr Richard Mead

Mead (1673-1754) was one of the most eminent physicians of his age, and eventually one of the wealthiest. He was born in the house of his father, the vicar of Stepney, and when he embarked on his medical career practised in that parish, though by then his father had been ejected from the living for being a nonconformist. Mead's researches and publications brought him fame and, then the ultimate reward, a particular standing in the royal household where he was thought to have saved George I's daughter from death.

Mead, together with a very large collection of books, manuscripts, coins and gems, moved to Great Ormond Street, a house on the site of today's Children's Hospital. But he appears to have had a Chelsea country home. The historian Thomas Faulkner puts him in Paradise Row (now Royal Hospital Road), but Randall Davies places him at a house in Milman's Street.

100. *Karl Marx (see p.71).*

Oliver Messel

Messel (1904-78), artist and stage designer, spent much of his life in Chelsea. Born in London, his grandfather was the *Punch* artist Linley Sambourne, whose extravagantly furnished house in Kensington is today opened to the public. Messel, together with his friend Rex Whistler, studied at the Slade where he made an early reputation for making masks. This talent was spotted by the theatre entrepreneur, C B Cochrane, who employed him to make masks for his next revue.

Messel's fame rested on his imaginative and fantastic style, which rose above what was then conventional theatrical costume and scenery. So well known did he become that his name was almost as much a draw as the actors themselves, and his Oliver Messel Room at the Dorchester hotel was also a great critical success.

Messel lived at 16 Yeomans Row from 1929 to 1946, and then moved slightly over the Chelsea border to Pelham Place.

Methodists in Chelsea

Chelsea Farm (the site of Cremorne Gardens *qv*) was once the London home of the 9th Earl of Huntingdon, Theophilus Hastings, and his wife Selina (1707-1791), though their main home was Castle Donnington. Selina was an early convert to Methodism, having attended meetings at the Fetter Lane address where the sect evolved. She was a member of the first Methodist society, formed in 1739 and had an influential friendship with the Wesley brothers. She disapproved of their interest in the Moravian sect *(qv)*, which settled in Cheyne Walk in 1751, and became herself a patron of itinerant preachers. Pouring her own money into the movement, she established about sixty chapels, used by preachers of her choosing, so that a 'Countess of Huntingdon Connexion' was established, almost as a distinct sect from mainstream Methodism. George Whitefield, then the most famous and persuasive of preachers, was her protégé.

At about that time the rector of Chelsea was the Rev. William Bromley Cadogan, an enthusiastic supporter of Whitefield, and his pulpit was often used by leading preachers of the Methodist persuasion, including John Wesley himself.

A local minister in 1813 fitted up a Huntingdon Connexion chapel in what remained of Ranelagh House. The congregation later moved to a street near Sloane Square to a site once occupied by a slaughter house – this Ranelagh Chapel later became the first home of the Royal Court Theatre *(qv)*.

Local Methodists also built a new chapel in Justice Walk with a schoolroom beneath. Here, Queen Victoria once attended, and Peter Jones the draper, and Thomas Carlyle were occasional members of the congregation. Early in the 20th century this congregation moved to the corner of Manor Street and King's Road, to a building that was badly damaged in the last war. When the site was redeveloped in the 1970s, a fundraising scheme (with the support of local resident Margaret Thatcher), raised £1 million to build a new church and pastoral centre, together with 21 homes for the elderly.

A A Milne

Alan Alexander Milne (1882-1956) became a famous children's author, but his early work was in journalism – he was assistant editor of *Punch* at the age of 24. He lived in two houses in Mallord Street. In 1920 he moved into no. 11 and from 1925 to *c*.1929 he was at no. 13. It was during this period that he wrote his most famous works. In 1924 he produced *When we were very young*, a series of verses for children, dedicated to his 4-year-old son Christopher Robin. *Winnie the Pooh*, followed in 1926, *Now we are six* in 1927 and *House at Pooh Corner* in 1928.

Naomi Mitchison

Naomi Mitchison (1897-1999) was a prolific writer in a very long and active life. She married in 1916 and spent much of the first five years of her marriage at 17 Cheyne Walk. Her first book (she wrote about eighty) appeared in 1923 – this was *The Conquered*, based on her wartime experiences.

She wrote in a variety of genres and one of her books, *We Have been Wanted* (1935), a then controversial study of sexual behaviour, was rejected by a number of publishers and censored once it did appear in print. She was a lifelong Socialist and feminist and travelled extensively: the Bakgatia tribe of Botswana adopted her as their adviser and Mother.

101. A A Milne

The Moravians

The Moravian protestant sect began with the United Brethren Church, founded in Czechoslovakia by John Huss in the 1400s, mainly in the areas of Moravia and Bohemia. Opposed to the corruption evident to them in the Catholic church, the sect was a precursor of the Protestant reformation. In 1457 it functioned as a reform wing of the Catholic church and ten years later broke away and began to ordain its own ministers.

Needless to say, persecution followed for many years. The sect was re-established in Germany in 1722 when they were housed by Count Nicholas Zinzendorf, and soon it spread to other parts of the world, notably Georgia in north America where there are still a substantial number of adherents.

In 1749 the Moravians were allowed to settle in England and to this end Count Zinzendorf bought Lindsey House (*qv*) in Cheyne Walk in 1751, which was used to board followers, while local stables were converted into a chapel.

Segregation of the sexes was required, even in death. In the Moravian burial ground in Milman's Street men and women were buried in separate parts of the ground, and even then married and unmarried people were kept apart.

The sect's residence in Chelsea was short-lived. Money ran out after Zinzendorf's death in 1760 and by 1770 the Moravians had left, though the burial ground remains today.

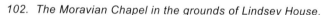
102. The Moravian Chapel in the grounds of Lindsey House.

103. *Sir Thomas More. Hand coloured etching c.1750-75, by Richard Dalton, after Hans Holbein the Younger.*

Sir Thomas More

More (1478-1535) is the illustrious name most closely associated with early Chelsea. He had a rapid rise in the turbulent times of Henry VIII, and an even faster decline. Destined as a youth for the law, he was appointed page at Lambeth Palace in the household of the Archbishop of Canterbury. He married Jane Colt in 1505, who bore him four children in quick succession, but who died in 1509. He remarried a widow, Alice Middleton, who was a strong supporter in the very troubled years to come. Still pursuing his legal career, he also wrote *Utopia* (publ. 1516), in which he assessed humanist principles and their conflict with religious dogma. His tolerance of unorthodox thinking did not survive his climb up the establishment ladder, and in particular he pursued William Tyndale, the translator of the Bible into English. The saintly More described the pious and learned Tyndale as 'a beste' with a 'brutysh bestely mouth' and insisted that Tyndale should be burned at the stake for heresy.

More was appointed Under Treasurer to Henry VIII in 1520 when Cardinal Wolsey was the chief of the king's advisers.

About 1525 More purchased 23 acres of land in Chelsea and built himself a large house by the river *(see illustration 14)*, in which he and his large family settled happily and in receipt of numerous distinguished visitors, including the artist Hans Holbein who not only illustrated *Utopia* but painted the More family group. The original painting, about 12ft x 9ft, is thought to have been lost in a fire in Moravia in 1792, but the family did have copies made – one is at the National Portrait Gallery (which includes a number of More's descendants as well) and another, acquired after fund raising by the Chelsea Society and the British Federation of Women Graduates' Charitable Foundation, is now hung at Chelsea Town Hall.

More followed Wolsey as Lord Chancellor in 1529 after the latter's death in disgrace over the matter of the king's divorce from Catherine of Aragon. However, More had strong reservations about the divorce and resigned the Chancellorship in 1532, retiring to Chelsea. When pressed he also opposed the dis-

104. Sir Thomas More, his family and servants. A sketch for a painting by Holbein which was lost in a fire in the 18th century. Copies were made before this disaster and one such is now hung in Chelsea Town Hall.

105. *Sir Thomas More's tomb in Chelsea Old Church.*

106. *Wolfgang Amadeus Mozart, portrait by Pietro Lorenzoni in 1763, a year before he came to London.*

were staying in Covent Garden, but on 6 August that year they moved to Ebury Street, then a rural location that Mozart delighted in. It was at this address he wrote two of his symphonies, K16 and K19.

solution of the monasteries and the king's assumption of the title of Supreme Head of the Church in England. No-one so prominent as More could escape retribution for his opposition, and in 1534 he was arrested at Chelsea and taken to the Tower. He was executed in 1535.

More's severed head was rescued by his daughter, Margaret Roper, and buried at St Dunstan's, Canterbury. His body was probably interred at the church of St Peter ad Vincula by the Tower, and there is no evidence that it was subsequently placed in the More tomb in Chelsea Old Church. More was canonised 400 years after his death.

The household was a large one at Chelsea. It included three married daughters and their husbands, eleven grandchildren, and a poor relation whom More

had adopted. 'There is not a man living so affectionate to his children as he', Erasmus wrote, 'he loveth his old wife as well as if she was a young maid' – a sure statement from someone who appears not to have visited More at Chelsea.

Wolfgang Amadeus Mozart

The prodigiously talented Mozart (1756-1791) stayed in London in the years 1764/5 together with his father, mother and sister. On 29 June 1764, then aged eight (but advertised as seven) he performed on the harpsichord and organ at the Ranelagh Rotunda (*qv*) in Chelsea. Most likely he was accompanied on the violin by his father. At that time the Mozart family

Alfred Munnings

Sir Alfred Munnings (1878-1959) was an unlikely Chelsea artist. He was not bohemian and detested modern art, usually making headlines when he voiced his opinions. What Munnings truly liked was painting horses, and this he did very well indeed – they made him a rich man. He was mainly in vogue between the wars and was elected President of the Royal Academy in 1944. In the vote for the office he defeated fellow Chelsea resident Augustus John. Munnings was, however, a totally inappropriate choice. He had no patience with meetings, no command of paper work, no interest in finance, and no ability to smooth ruffled feathers. Whether Augustus John would have done any better is open to question.

Munnings resigned the Presidency in 1949, but continued to repeat his criticism of 'modern' artists. His popularity waned as his style of traditional painting lost its appeal, but in recent years his pictures have sold very well, particularly those featuring horses.

He lived from 1920 until his death at 96 Chelsea Park Gardens.

National Army Museum

This Museum, in Royal Hospital Road, was established in 1961 to display the history of the British Army from the reign of Henry VII – its material carries through to recent wars involving British troops. The first building phase, designed by William Holford & Partners, was completed in 1971 and additional facilities have followed. The museum's collections include numerous uniforms, 40,000 books, 25,000 prints and drawings and 500,000 photographs.

It is open every day, 10-5.30, except on public holidays.

James Camden Neild

Neild (c.1780-1852) was a Chelsea eccentric, but not an attractive one. He lived at no. 5 Cheyne Walk, where his philanthropic father, a retired jeweller, had moved in 1792. Neild senior died in 1814 leaving his fortune and house to his son, James Camden Neild, who lived the life of a recluse until his own death in 1852. He was also a miser to himself. He had very little furniture in the house and, according to the *Dictionary of National Biography*, for some time he had no bed to lie in. He wore, the *Biography* goes on to say, a blue swallow-tailed coat with gilt buttons, brown trousers and patched shoes. He never allowed his clothes to be brushed because he maintained that took the nap off them.

Neild walked everywhere if possible, unwilling to spend money on cabs, and in the interest of accumulating money he visited his estates and properties personally, staying with tenants to save hotel charges and sharing their modest fare. Obviously of a very depressed nature, he attempted suicide in 1828.

On his death he left £500,000 as a personal gift to Queen Victoria. On receiving the news, Victoria's uncle Leopold remarked that it was very good news 'because one never knew what might happen to Royalty which was already much diminished on the Continent.' For her part, Victoria erected a stained glass window in Neild's memory in North Marston church, a village in which he owned property and where he spent much of the latter part of his life.

107. *The National Army Museum in Royal Hospital Road.*

Newspapers

Numerous newspapers have been published for Chelsea residents but few have had staying power. A continuous thread may be deduced for the *Chelsea News*, which seems to have its roots in the *West London Times* (covering Kensington and Chelsea) from 1860-7. This appears to have become the *West London Press* serving the same area which, in 1885, became the *Westminster and Chelsea News*. Its descendant, the *Chelsea News*, has been published since 1972 and the *Kensington and Chelsea Times* has appeared since 1983.

Nursery Gardens

A good many acres of west London were once covered by market and nursery gardens, the first to supply fresh food to central London, the second to accommodate a growing appetite for foreign plants. George Bryan in his book on Chelsea in 1869 remarked that 'the line of the [King's] Road was almost exclusively occupied by nurserymen and florists, and thus it became a fashionable resort for the nobility and gentry.' There was a great deal of competition from gardens at Fulham and Hammersmith, and in earlier times from the first significant nursery garden, the Brompton Park Nurseries, part of whose site was used to build the Victoria & Albert Museum.

The largest Chelsea business was the Exotic Nursery, between the Fulham Road and King's Road, bounded west and east by Hortensia Road and Gunter Grove. This was founded in 1808 by Joseph Knight, a keen collector of plants who travelled annually to the continent to import specimens and who bought as a matter of course from Brazil and China. The business grew enormously and his nephew John Perry joined him as a partner.

Knight died in 1855 possessed of a good fortune, the business having been sold two years earlier to the Scots nurseryman John Veitch. The number and variety of plants and the space they occupied grew even larger – more land was taken on the south side of the King's Road to accommodate this expansion. The gardening press was very impressed by Veitch's efficiency and stock. They also commented on the fact that he employed trainees and paid them a pittance, but he taught them so well that they were able to obtain jobs easily on private estates simply because they had been trained by him.

But development of valuable Chelsea land inevitably loomed, and the business was sold in 1914 to make room for streets.

The other important nursery in Chelsea – there had been at least 25 concerns since the 1750s – was Colvill's, which had two grounds on the King's Road, one by Blacklands Terrace and the

108. *Oakley Street from the King's Road, painted c.1890 by William B Huse.*

other east of Sloane Square. There was a bizarre happening in 1826, when Colvill's foreman in charge of exotic plants, Robert Sweet, was accused of receiving a few plants which had been stolen from Kew Gardens. This seemed an unlikely charge, since Sweet had no pecuniary gain from the sale of plants at Colvill's, and many eminent people vouched for his character in court. The charge was more serious than on the surface, for to steal from the king (the owner of Kew Gardens) was a capital offence. Sweet was found not guilty, but he retired from Colvill's and spent much of the rest of his years writing books about plants.

Bacon's map of London for 1888 shows some nursery gardens still left in Chelsea. Apart from that of Veitch, there were two in the Lots Road area, and one to the east of Beaufort Street.

Oakley Street

This street was formed when Winchester House *(qv)*, the previous London home of the bishops of Winchester, was demolished in 1822. The street's name derives from the Cadogan family – William Cadogan was created Baron Cadogan of Oakley in 1718.

Illustrious residents have included E F Benson, writer (1867-1940) at no 10 in 1920 before he moved on to Brompton Square *c.*1923; the sculptor Elisabeth Frink (1930-93) at no. 93 by 1954 until *c.*1960; the character actor Richard Goolden at no. 15 by 1967 to at least 1972; the composer Percy Grainger (1882-1961) in 1903, having moved there from Coulson Street. He went on to live at 14 Upper Cheyne Row 1905-7 and 31a King's Road 1908-14; the ill-fated explorer, Robert Scott

(1868-1912), who was at no. 56 in 1905-8. The spy, Donald Maclean, also lived in the street. Round the corner at 33 Oakley Gardens lived the writer George Gissing from 1882-4.

Old Church Street

From its location next to the ancient parish church, and its appearance on the earliest maps, it may be assumed that Old Church Street is the oldest street in Chelsea. It extends from the Fulham Road to Cheyne Walk, although in the seventeenth century the section north of King's Road was merely called 'the Road to the Cross Tree', possibly indicating a wayside pulpit at the northern end.

Famous residents have included John Betjeman, the poet, (1906-84) at no. 53 from 1917-24; the actress Constance Cummings at no. 66 by 1947 to at least 1967; Evelyn Pickering, artist (1855-1919) at no. 127 from 1910-19 *(see separate entry for William de Morgan)*; Anthony Gross, artist (1905-1984) at no. 137 by 1948 to at least 1958; Adrian Jones,

sculptor (1845-1938), at no. 147 from 1892-1937); Charles Kingsley the writer (1819-1875), at no. 56 1836-1860 (his father was Chelsea's rector); the peripatetic Katherine Mansfield (1888-1923) at no. 141a in 1917; Edward Maufe, architect (1883-1974) at no. 139 by 1962; the writer Robert Ross (1869-1918) at no. 54 in 1892; Jonathan Swift (1667-1745) in 1711 and Charles Wheeler, sculptor (1892-1974) at Hereford Buildings.

The southern end of the street suffered severe damage during the last war when the Old Church was all but destroyed. In 2002 a new church hall was built, designed by John Simpson.

Not many modern houses exist in the street. An intrusive development stands opposite the Rectory, but there are two notable 1930s' buildings: no. 64 by Mendelssohn and Chermayeff, and no. 66 by Gropius and Fry.

An outstanding terrace of early nineteenth-century houses is at nos 129-139. No. 149 used to be an asylum for ladies suffering 'from the milder forms of mental disease'.

109. No 46 Old Church Street, formerly Wright's Dairy, in 2003.

110. No. 49 Old Church Street, the frontage to Hereford Buildings.

111. Old Church Street, photographed by James Hedderley, probably in the late1870s.

112. Justice Walk, seen from Old Church Street, with Lawrence Street in the distance, 2003.

113. The new church hall, designed by John Simpson, opened in 2002.

114. *Ormonde House, a drawing by M J Rush.*

Ormonde House

Ormonde House was at the junction of Paradise Row (now Royal Hospital Road) and Smith Street – Ormonde Gate now commemorates its location. It is possible that the house was built *c*.1664, as the 1st Duke of Ormonde had a connection with Chelsea that year. Minor aristocrats occupied the house for another one hundred years until in 1777 it was taken by the 'Maritime School', founded here to train scholars to be naval officers. It was, so a pamphlet described, 'truly on the banks of the Thames, being in Paradise Row, Chelsea, on the waterside, on a fair, healthy, detached spot. It is an old house properly cleansed and fitted up, to contain twenty-six scholars with the several officers and servants who are necessary to reside in the house.' A special feature of the education was that the pupils erected in the yard at the back a fully-rigged vessel large enough to permit 24 cadets to have climbing practice. This vessel was duly christened the Cumberland, after the institution's president, the Duke of Cumberland. Pupils leaving (at the age of 14) were encouraged to have 'religion, peaceableness, good humour, purity of speech and discipline'.

The proprietor, John Battesworth, taught maths and navigation, but one suspects that the guiding hand was that of the philanthropist Jonas Hanway (who also popularised the invention of the umbrella), and who went on to found the Marine Society with the aim of training destitute boys for the navy.

115. *Paradise Row, from a drawing by W W Burgess.*

Paradise Row

Paradise Row is now that part of Royal Hospital Road to the south-west of Smith Street. It was once a much-loved array of rather run-down but pictur-esque houses and shops. The last remnants were destroyed in 1906, to the dismay of old Chel-sea residents, in particular Reginald Blunt (*qv*) who, in 1927, when he founded the Chelsea Society, was determined not to let such wanton destruc-tion happen again. In those days, with far fewer planning controls, a land owner, in this case the Cadogans, could do much as it wanted. Blunt was moved to write a book about Paradise Row, and poignantly sums up the circumstances for destruction in a way that can still be relevant if there are not safeguards:

'One knows only too well the usual course of events – there is something tragic-comi-cal about it – when the doom of some interesting old place looms imminent. The rumour passes round that it is to go; and people say "How sad!" or "How iniquitous!" or "About time, too!" according to their bent of mind. But nobody does anything, and for a while noth-ing happens, and the report is forgotten. Then, one by one the tenants vanish and are not re-placed; and when the poor old windows have grown dirty enough little boys begin throw-ing big stones through them. Then suddenly, one fine morn-ing, behold a hoarding and housebreakers and pickaxes at work. And now there is much bluster and turmoil. Somebody writes to *The Times*, indignation is poured forth by columns, various good people promul-gate sketch suggestions as to what might and should have been done. the office topo-graphical shelf is ransacked, and paragraphs result with a more or less hackneyed rechauffe of the history of the place, and a headline or two about landlords and vandal-ism. Meanwhile the navvy and the pickaxe are merrily master-ing the situation, and by the time that precious entity, the man in the street, has been awakened to some momentary interest in the matter, a pile of bricks and shattered timber is all that remains on which to focus his energies. And so with a shrug he passes on and for-gets, as soon as may be.'

In the case of Paradise Row local residents were a little more active than this, but the Cadogan Estate pressed on with its plans, and many fine late 17th-century houses were demolished. The oldest properties, shown on Hamilton's map of 1677, were those knocked down in 1906.

Park Chapel

This privately owned chapel at the corner of Park Walk and Chelsea Park Gardens was built in 1718 at the expense of Sir Richard Massingham. Its minis-ter in 1812 was involved in the founding of the missionary British and Foreign Bible Soci-ety. The Chapel and its infant school were closed in 1913.

116. Paradise Row, from a watercolour by G Munson.

Peter Jones

Peter Rees Jones (1843-1905) was apprenticed to a draper in Carmarthen before coming to London to set up his own business. He began in Hackney, moved on to Bloomsbury and then took two shops in Draycott Avenue which opened as a 'Co-operative Drapery'. But disaster happened here, for while the two shops were being knocked through into one, walls collapsed and an apprentice was killed and his own wife buried, though she survived. In 1877 he took over 4-6 King's Road and gradually expanded into other properties adjacent – eventually he had twelve in the row and 200 employees. It was a typical expansion in Victorian times, repeated in many high streets, as drapers, thriving on the fashion for drapes and voluminous clothes, added shop after shop until it was possible to redevelop them as a single unit. This Jones did in the 1880s with a red brick and stone building. It had a green slate roof, the interior was lit by electricity and there were walnut and ebony showcases. As was usual at that time, the better class houses in the district were delivered to, and Peter Jones kept nine horse-drawn vans in a stable at Rawlings Street. Many of his staff lived in premises supplied by the management. In 1900 Jones registered the business as a private company – his annual turnover was £180,000.

Difficult trading conditions coincided with the death of Peter Jones in 1905, and it was another and more successful draper who bought the business. John Lewis of Oxford Street had the inestimable advantage of his shop being on the Central Line. Legend has it that he took a bus down (or walked in some ver-

117. The Peter Jones shop in the late 1930s.

sions) to Sloane Square, with £20,000 in his pocket to buy the store.

The Chelsea shop was fortunate in that John Lewis's son, John Spedan Lewis, was put in charge of the store at the age of 21 in 1906. Spedan Lewis had a rare conscience about his staff and in times to come was to be at odds with his father in this matter. Spedan Lewis recalls:

'It was soon clear to me that my father's success had been due to his trying constantly to give very good value to people who wished to exchange their money for his merchandise; but it also became clear to me that the business would have grown further, and that my father's life would have been much happier, if he had done the same for those who wished to exchange their work for his money.

The profit, even after ten thousand pounds had been set aside as interest at 5 per cent upon the capital, was equal to the whole of the pay of the staff, of whom there were about three hundred.

To his two children my father seemed to have all that anyone could want. Yet for years he

had been spending no more than a small fraction of his income. On the other hand, for very nearly all of his staff any saving worth mentioning was impossible.'

It was Spedan Lewis who turned the whole John Lewis empire into a profit-sharing partnership in 1929.

The Peter Jones shop was rebuilt in 1932-6 to the designs of Slater, Crabtree and Moberly, with Professor C H Reilly as associate architect. *The Times* was enthusiastic:

'A building which gives so much pleasure and entertainment as to make one feel that there must be a catch in it somewhere, is the new Peter Jones... It is, in effect a glass cage, rounding into the Square on a double curve, the ground floor affording an uninterrupted display, under cover, against a cyclorama background... a principle of construction... that can only be called revolutionary.'

The Chelsea Society retorted very sniffily:

'This frankly expressed modernist view of Chelsea's

latest architectural acquisition must be left to the acceptance or rejection of our members; but without throwing stones at Peter Jones' 'glass cage' it may be pointed out that for all its glassiness the ground floor is entirely dependent upon artificial light; and that, to many of us, the look of stability in the mushroom construction of the cantilevered front is by no means obvious... If we must have glass cages, they should surely at least give their inmates daylight.'

The store at the moment is undergoing substantial alteration.

Petyt School

In 1705 Chelsea Vestry authorised William Petyt, a resident of Chelsea and Keeper of the Records at the Tower of London, to rebuild the parish school at his own expense. The site, adjoining the old churchyard, had previously contained a house for the parish clerk and a schoolhouse built while Dr Richard Ward was Rector (1585-1615). Petyt's new school comprised a vestry room on the ground floor, a schoolroom at first floor level, and rooms for the schoolmaster above that. But the building was small – 28 feet x 26 feet.

The purpose of the school was defined as 'The Education of Poor Children in the knowledge and practice of the Christian religion ....' It was the custom twice each Sunday for the scholars to be ranged in the cloister 'with their caps off and there to stand until the congregation be passed by' and they were to 'be given to understand who are their Benefactors and instructed that as often as they pass by any of them they pull off their caps and make them a bow.' On the other hand, the demands on the schoolmaster were more stringent. He had to

118. Petyt House, from an engraving by W W Burgess.

'frequent Holy Communion, govern himself and his passions, write a good hand, understand the grounds of arithmetic, and keep good order in his own family.' He was not allowed to whip the children except in the presence of one or more of the governors or trustees who had 'the power to hear and examine the crime and remit the punishment'.

By 1819 over a hundred boys and girls were being clothed and educated free. The girls then moved to a house in Lordship Lane and in c.1825, when new schools were built in the King's Road, the old school building became a fire station, and later a mission hall. It was rebuilt in 1890 as a Church House, but destroyed by the bomb that so damaged the church itself in 1941.

The Pheasantry

No. 152 King's Road is a Pizza Express which, after a long unoccupied period of desolation and uncertainty succeeded one of Chelsea's famous institutions, The Pheasantry.

The present building is an enlargement of one that first appears on a map in 1769. Nesta Macdonald, who has done much research on this property and from whose booklet on the subject much of this information is derived, notes that four families dominated its earlier years, Baker, Evans, Markham and Joubert, of which the Jouberts were to be more significant in the house's history. Ms Macdonald has found an advertisement placed in *The Field* in April 1865 by the Baker family, who had premises in Beaufort Street:

119. *The Pheasantry in its heyday.*

120. *The Pheasantry in King's Road, 2003, now a Pizza Express.*

'PHEASANTS Messrs. Baker beg to invite their patrons, customers, and gentlemen interested in the breed of PHEASANTS to an INSPECTION at their new Establishment, 152 King's Road, Chelsea, of Specimens of the different varieties of the BREEDING STOCK, conspicuous amongst which will be the Versicolor or Japanese Pheasants, with first and second cross, which cannot fail to be interesting to all desirous of improving the breed.'

Thus, the advent of the Baker business here explains and dates the name of The Pheasantry.

In 1881 the premises were acquired by the Joubert family, descendants of highly-skilled upholsterers from France. Jean-Baptiste set up his business in Maddox Street in the West End in 1830-1 and the family later made reproduction furniture and parquet flooring. The Jouberts moved to Chelsea at the same time as the Cadogan developments, including Cadogan Square, were taking place. The affluent families then flowing into Chelsea needed the expertise of the Jouberts to enhance their spacious apartments and houses.

Despite the house and its outbuildings being used for the business, the Jouberts let out the main floor in 1916 to the Russian Princess Serafine Astafieva, a relative of Tolstoy. The Princess was a ballet dancer and in 1909 performed with Diaghilev's company in Paris and in London in 1911. She came back to England in 1914, began a Russian Dancing Academy, and then in 1916 moved it into The Pheasantry where she was highly successful as a teacher – Anna Neagle was one of her pupils, but more famously as dancers were Anton Dolin, Alicia Markova and Margot Fonteyn. Diaghilev was a frequent visitor to the house.

In 1932 the last of the Jouberts retired and The Pheasantry property was then run by an Italian Réné de Meo, who turned the basement into a club-restaurant. This very special place lasted for thirty-five years and its members included Augustus John, Pietro Annigoni, and many people in the arts generally. Subscriptions were suitably graded: artists 10/6d, ladies 15/- and gentlemen 1 guinea. Ms Macdonald lists some of those who used it: Francis Bacon, Aneurin Bevan, Chagall, Cyril Connolly, Lucien Freud, Gigli, Robert Newton, Gregory Peck, John Rothenstein, Dylan Thomas, Peter Ustinov....

The most expensive dish on a 1954 menu was seven shillings for a veal escalope.

De Meo had a heart attack in 1958 and the business was carried on by his partner, Mario Cazzini, until his death in 1966. The club did not long survive him and there then followed a very long period of uncertainty as to the future of the property. The freehold was owned by the Cadogan Estate and there was a very real danger in the 1970s that the house would be demolished. Nesta Macdonald was in the forefront of the campaign which saved it.

121. *Dr Phené*

Dr Phené

An extraordinary house was built in Oakley Street as from 1901, a vast pile, resembling a French chateau, with numerous pillars and ornamental figures on its decorative face, painted and gilded, as Barbara Denny puts it, like a grubby wedding cake. It was the creation of another Chelsea eccentric, Dr John Samuel Phené (1823-1912), an architect and antiquarian who himself lived at 32 Oakley Street. Phené had strong views about a number of things, one of which has been borne out since, that planting trees in streets helps to reduce pollution. As he developed much of Oakley Street he carried out his idea there with the result that the street was one of the first in Chelsea to be planted – the pictures of Tite Street and Sydney Street elsewhere in this book show just how bare of trees were Chelsea streets of this period.

Phené collected a vast assembly of architectural and archaeological items, many of which were displayed in his garden.

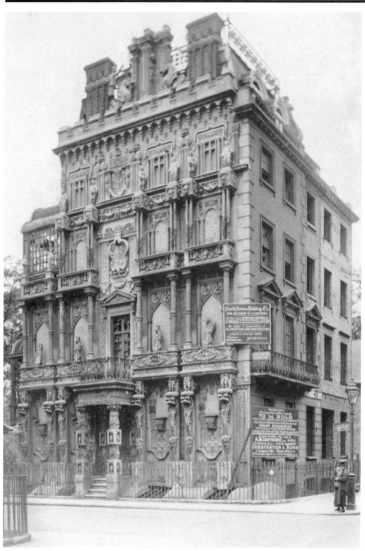

122. *Dr Phené's 'chateau' in Chelsea.*

plants which could ease or halt diseases or physical disabilities. This led to the additional use of the land at Chelsea to grow herbs, a modest enough venture until Sir Hans Sloane bought the manor of Chelsea and lived nearby. Sloane was interested in the project and was keen to have the Garden expand. He granted the Apothecaries the freehold of the land provided that it presented to the Royal Society each year fifty new plants, until the number had reached 2000. The Company, in gratitude, commissioned Rysbrack to sculpt a statue of Sloane to be placed in the Garden in 1737.

John Evelyn, inevitably, was a visitor here. In his diary for 7 August 1685, he records:

'I went to see Mr Watts, keeper of the Apothe-caries Garden of Simples at Chelsea, where there is a collection of innumerable rarities of that sort, particularly, besides many rare annuals, the tree bearing jesuit's bark, which had done such wonders in quartan agues. What was very ingenious was the subterranean heat, conveyed by a stove under the conservatory, all vaulted with brick, so as he has the doors and windows open in the hardest frost, secluding only the snow.'

Note here the early use of a greenhouse.

The most important stewardship of the Garden in its earlier years was that of Philip Miller, who was appointed in 1722 and stayed for nearly fifty years, raising the reputation of the Garden to international level. One of his assistants was William Aitken, who later became one of the first managers of Kew Gardens. The botanist Linnaeus visited the Garden in 1736.

A feature of the Garden, which may be seen in the 1751

But he also determined to build a replica of the Chateau de Savenay on the Loire, which his family had once owned and which was destroyed in a Royalist uprising in the 1790s. Phené himself was a recluse and did not live in this replica, and it is difficult to understand his reason for expending so much of his fortune on its construction. In any event, it did not last long for the house was demolished in 1917.

The Physic Garden

About ten years before the foundation stone of the Royal Hospital was laid, to its east the Apothecaries' Company acquired in 1673 a piece of land on the Chelsea riverside on which to construct a boat house for its ceremonial barge. They took on a 61-year lease at £5 per annum from the lord of the manor, Charles Cheyne. Apothecaries were particularly interested in the properties of herbs and other

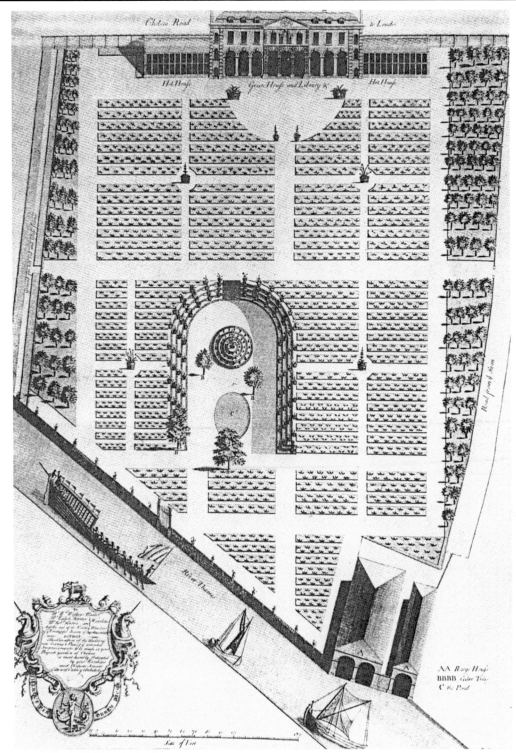

123. The new layout for the Physic Garden adopted during the 1730s. The famous Cedars of Lebanon trees are towards the centre.

124. *The Physic Garden from the river, showing the Cedars of Lebanon.*

plan illustrated here, were the two Cedars of Lebanon *(see illustrations 123 and 124)*. These were planted as 3-foot saplings in 1683 and grew to be about 15 feet in girth. Unfortunately they no longer survive.

Within the grounds is the oldest rock garden in the country, constructed of stone from the Tower of London.

The nineteenth century brought many problems, not the least being the gradual increase in manufactured medicine, which made botanic treatment seem antiquated and less effective. Another trouble was the pollution of the area, with smoke drifting over from the power stations at Battersea and Lots Road.

In 1990 it was rumoured that the Apothecaries were to sell off their land at Chelsea for development. A protest meeting was held at Chelsea Town Hall and resistance was formulated. The government was enticed into financial help, but only if students from the Royal College of Science at South Kensington had use of the Garden. In the 1980s a trust was set up to ensure the future of the oldest existing botanical garden in the country.

Princes Sports Club

This apparently regal club, but actually named after the Prince brothers who began it, was housed in the 1870s on part of the grounds of Henry Holland's house, The Pavilion, in Hans Town *(qv)*. Its cricket pitch was highly recommended by *Wisden* and the MCC used it before moving on to Lords. Other sports were added – tennis, badminton and ice skating. Women were allowed as members, but only if they had been presented at Court. In 1885 the club moved to West Kensington, where it became the Queens Club.

Public Houses

Chelsea has been blessed with many public houses, some with wonderful views across the river. Those near the Thames have mostly disappeared, some to the creation of the Embankment in the 1870s, others lost as trade moved northwards to the King's Road area, and others, such as the King's Head and Eight Bells on Cheyne Walk, simply to change of use. The Cross Keys in Lawrence Street, its face adorned with some confusing swans, survives, but it is not now the quiet neighbourhood pub of less frenetic days.

Others have changed their name. The famous Six Bells in the King's Road is now Henry J. Bean, the Black Lion in Old Church Street is the Front Page. However, the Edwardian version of the World's End Tavern managed to survive the wholesale council development in that area.

125. *The White Horse, formerly in Old Church Street, c.1820.*

126. *The garden front of the Six Bells, now the Henry J. Bean, in King's Road c.1912.*

127. *The Royal Hospital Tavern; drawing by Walter Greaves. This pub, at the junction of Franklin's Row and Royal Hospital Road, was replaced by flats.*

Ranelagh Gardens

The 18th-century pleasure ground, Ranelagh Gardens, was located south of today's Royal Hospital Museum.

Richard Jones, the 1st Earl of Ranelagh, appointed Paymaster General of the Royal Hospital in 1685, contrived to build himself a handsome house on the hospital's grounds. He was a surprising choice for someone to take charge of funds, for he was on the verge of bankruptcy and was described at the time as a 'man of great parts and great vices, a person who loved his ease and his belly and all sorts of pleasures and most profuse therein'. Inevitably, he took advantage of his position, though later found innocent of corruption – indeed he was granted the 20-acre site of the house and grounds in perpetuity. Jones proceeded with more profligacy, creating walks, pools, orchards,

128. *View of the Rotunda at Ranelagh, published in 1770.*

an aviary, a bathing house and statues, until in 1702 he was found guilty of gross fraud to the extent of £72,000 and dismissed from his post, though little could be done about his ownership of the house. This corruption did not appear to dis-may him or his family and they continued to entertain on a lavish scale. After his death his daughter once entertained George I here, engaging Handel and a 50-strong orchestra for a performance of his *Water Music* on one of the flotilla of boats ferrying the guests to her garden.

By 1741 the house and grounds were in other hands. A company headed by Sir William Robinson decided to convert the premises to be a rival to Vaux-hall Gardens. The grounds were laid out in spectacular fashion

ing month he described the amphitheatre again as 'finely gilt, painted and illuminated; into which everybody that loves eating, drinking, staring or crowding, is admitted for twelvepence.' In 1748 there was an early traffic jam when Walpole complained that 'Ranelagh is so crowded, that going there t'other night in a string of coaches, we had a stop of six and thirty minutes.'

The circumference of the Rotunda was 555 feet, with an internal diameter 150 feet, much the same as the Reading Room at the British Museum. It was entered through four Doric doors. There were 52 boxes – each decorated with a painting and provided with candles – in which seven or eight people could be seated. Above these was another gallery of boxes. Much of the construction of this vast building was of wood, but unusually, it never did burn down despite the fact that there was an open fireplace and a chimney in the centre of it.

The usual entry charge was half a crown, which included tea, coffee, bread and butter and, it seems, whatever entertainments were available.. It was not riotous. Samuel Rogers in 1786 records that 'all was so orderly and still that you could hear the whishing sound of the ladies' trains as the immense assembly walked round and round the room.' He went on to say that he had arrived there in a coach with a lady who had to sit on a stool in the coach because her head dress was too high to sit on a normal seat. Other entertainments, apart from the promenade around the Rotunda, included concerts, fireworks, dancing and concerts. In 1749 a masquerade was held to celebrate the Peace Treaty of Aix la Chapelle, which Walpole de-

but the sensational centrepiece was the Rotunda, an amphitheatre designed by William Jones, the architect to the East India Company. This opened to the public on 5 April 1742, a month ahead of the gardens. Horace Walpole remarked that

month: 'I have been breakfasting this morning at Ranelagh Garden: they have built an immense amphitheatre, with balconies full of little alehouses.: it is in rivalry to Vauxhall and costs above twelve thousand pounds.' The follow-

129. *Interior of the Rotunda at Ranelagh.*

scribed as 'the best understood and the prettiest spectacle that I ever saw, nothing in a fairy-tale ever surpassed it.'

There were also balloon ascents. One in 1802 celebrated the Peace of Amiens, when the luckless astronauts drifted off to Colchester, where they made a crash landing. By 1826 Ranelagh was closed and the site sold to the Royal Hospital.

Dante Gabriel Rossetti

Rossetti (1828-82) ranks with Turner and Augustus John as a 'Chelsea artist'. He moved into 16 Cheyne Walk (which is also referred to as Queen's House) in 1862, a vast house with twelve bedrooms and an acre of ground at the back. All for £110 a year, though it should be remembered that Thomas Carlyle,

round the corner in Cheyne Row, was paying only £30 per year. Rossetti seems to have wanted to establish some kind of commune of artists there, but this was not a success. His brother William did not stay long, nor did the poet Algernon Swinburne. The writer George Meredith, though invited, appears not to have taken up the offer, though Hall Caine came later and stayed.

Rossetti installed a small menagerie in the back garden, which included a kangaroo and peacocks and also an animal called a zebu, a form of ox. Indoors he kept mice and a wombat. Rossetti had a stroke in 1881 and died the following year at Birchington-on-Sea, in a villa owned by his friend, the architect J P Seddon.

Subsequent tenants at Cheyne Walk were specifically prohibited from keeping wombats.

130. *Dante Gabriel Rossetti.*

Royal Court Theatre

The New Chelsea Theatre opened in what is now Sloane Gardens in 1870 in the old Ranelagh Chapel. *The Era* magazine tells us:

'The crowded south western district of London not possessing anything like a theatre nearer than the Haymarket and St James's, it occurred to the gentlemen above named that a dissenting chapel (close by the aristocratic neighbourhood of Eaton Square) which had, perhaps been the means of converting thousands, might itself be advantageously converted – into a Theatre.'

But it was not to be, for the staple diet of comedies and light dramas was not what the public wanted, until in 1885 the theatre staged a series of popular Pinero farces. By the time of its demolition in 1887, due to the rebuilding of Sloane Square, the theatre was called the Royal Court.

The theatre's new building in Sloane Square opened on 24 September 1888 with a farcical comedy called *Mamma!*. It was designed by the theatre architects Walter Emden and Bertie Crewe, with a capacity of 841. There was a successful run under the management of

Granville Barker and J E Vedrenne, notable for the presentation of new playwrights such as Shaw and Galsworthy. *Heartbreak House* and *Back to Methusaleh*, by Shaw, both got their first nights here. From 1924 to 1927 Eden Phillpotts' *The Farmer's Wife* had an exceptionally long run, but the competition of cinema began to take its toll. In 1932 the theatre closed and as from 1935 the building was used as a cinema. It was bombed in 1940 but reopened as a theatre in 1953 under the management of the London Theatre Guild, which needed a

131. *The interior of the Royal Court Theatre in 1871.*

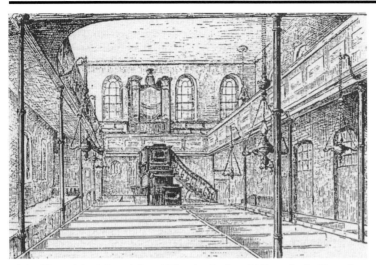

132. The original Royal Court Theatre in the old Ranelagh Chapel.

133. Programme for the first production of Heartbreak House by Shaw, at the Royal Court.

theatre to try out new dramatists. This was a considerable success, for their productions included *The Threepenny Opera* and *Airs on a Shoestring*.

The turning point in the theatre's career and reputation was in 1956 when George Devine and the English Stage Company took over. Their management saw first performances of John Osborne's *Look Back in Anger* and *The Entertainer*, as well as new plays by Wesker, Pinter and Beckett.

The theatre in recent years has continued Devine's adventurous policy. New plays are the staple fare, with playwrights such as the late Sarah Kane and Conor McPherson still jolting us out of our expectations.

Aided by Lottery money, the Royal Court has recently had a major overhaul. Which is just as well, for in 1994 its director, the young Stephen Daldry, recorded that 'The drains flood the understage and the stalls in winter just as they did in Shaw's day and the admin offices are a Dickensian rabbit warren, the stage machinery is hopelessly inefficient and the front of house facilities awful.'

The Royal Hospital

The establishment of a hospital and almshouses for soldiers wounded in war was both an ambition and an embarrassment for Charles II. He recognised that the country had a debt to pay, and he was particularly impressed during his exile in Paris with the Hôtel des Invalides, which performed the same function. But Charles II was hard-pressed during the earlier part of his reign, what with the Dutch wars and the afflictions of the Great Plague and Great Fire. Money was difficult to find.

The site at Chelsea, where a Theological College had once been located (*see Chelsea College*), and which the Royal Society had abortively made plans to use, was bought by the Crown for £13,000 with the help of the Paymaster General, Stephen Fox. The king laid the foundation stone in 1682 but did not live to see the scheme's completion. The majestic range of buildings we see today are mostly by Christopher Wren. The first inhabitants, 479 former soldiers, were admitted on 28 March 1689.

The Hospital has not changed much outwardly since it was opened. It is constructed around three courtyards, the main one, known as Figure Court, opening to the south and the other two to the east and west. Figure Court contains a statue of Charles II by Grinling Gibbons, in front of which the ex-soldiers march each year to commemorate the king's escape after the Battle of Worcester in 1651. A second statue, of an In-Pensioner, was unveiled in the grounds on 4 May 2000; this was paid for by the Duke of Westminster.

Particularly fine artworks within the Hospital are portraits in the Council Chamber of Charles I and his family by Van Dyck, and of Charles II, Catherine of Braganza, and the future James II, by Lely. The half-dome of the apse in the chapel was painted by Sebastiano Ricci and his nephew Marco.

The pensioners are mostly housed in the east and west sides of Figure Court. Their bedrooms on the upper floors are reached by shallow steps – a

134. Pensioners relaxing in the cloisters of the Royal Hospital early in the 20th century.

135. An In-Pensioner, by George Alsop.

feature provided by Wren so as not to tax rather aged limbs. The pensioners eat in the Great Hall, which is 115 feet long, 38 feet wide and 37 feet high. They are served before the officers of the Hospital as a mark of respect for their previous contribution to the country. As they eat they are reminded of their founder by a large mural of Charles II on horseback, begun by Verrio and completed by Henry Cooke. The pensioners' uniform – scarlet coats in the summer and blue in the winter – has remained virtually unchanged.

An early, but not cheering, provision at the hospital was a burial ground to the east of the main building. This was closed in 1854 and the pensioners were allocated a special plot in

136. Sir Robert Walpole, from a painting by J B Van Loo. (See p.98)

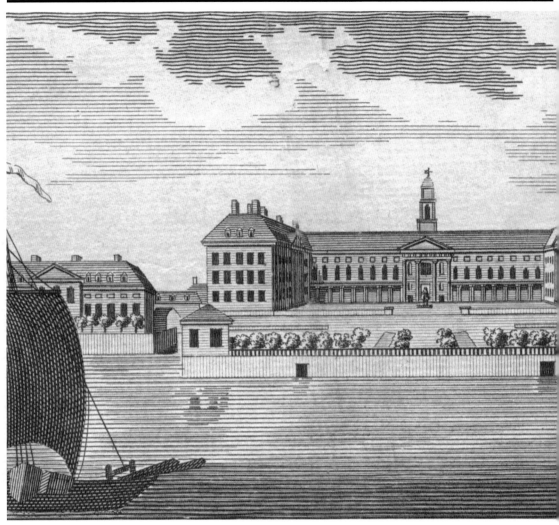

137. *The Royal Hospital at Chelsea, published 1770.*

Brompton Cemetery; nowadays they are interred at Brookwood in Surrey.

On the death of the Duke of Wellington in 1852, his body lay in state here. Such was the crowd on the first day to view the Duke that two people were crushed to death.

To the west of the Hospital stands a house which became the Hospital's Infirmary. This was previously the home of the prime minister, Robert Walpole. It was built on land originally leased at the end of the 17th century by the Hospital to William Jephson, Secretary to the Treasury. Walpole, who was also Paymaster-General of the Hospital. Walpole arrived *c.*1722 and lived at Chelsea in the summer months until his death in 1745.

The house was remodelled by Sir John Soane in 1810 and became an Infirmary to the Hospital. Another house was built in the garden nearer to the river, which eventually became a residence for the Infirmary staff.

The Infirmary was mostly destroyed by a landmine in 1941 and was rebuilt in 1961.

Nowadays there are between 350 and 400 pensioners, who are drawn from Out-pensioners over the age of 65.

The Hospital and its grounds (66 acres) are open to the public daily from 10-12 and 2-5, during which hours the Great Hall and the Chapel may be visited. Additionally, members of the public may attend chapel services on Sundays at 8.30am and 11am.

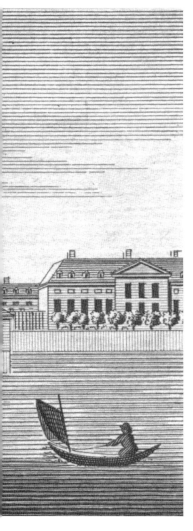

138. A war-disabled pensioner at the Royal Hospital

The Hospital's museum originated with a display in the Great Hall in 1866. In 1960 it was housed in the Secretary's Block. However, it has now been completely refurbished and enlarged. It contains a striking model of the Royal Hospital and its gardens as they would have appeared in 1742. The entrance hall is dedicated to the Duke of Wellington and there are a number of exhibits relating to him. There are also over 2000 medals, mainly bequeathed to the Hospital by former inmates or unclaimed on their death. There is also a reconstruction of a typical living quarter of a pensioner.

The Royal Marsden Hospital

This hospital, at the corner of Fulham Road and Dovehouse Street, was instituted in 1851 by William Marsden (1796-1867), who had already founded the Royal Free in 1828. Marsden was a remarkable man. He was born in Sheffield in 1796, apprenticed to a druggist, came to London and was in his own practice in Holborn by 1821; in 1827 he became a Member of the Royal College of Surgeons. The most repeated story about Marsden is that he came across a girl, very seriously ill, on the steps of St Andrew's Holborn and tried to get her into one of the large central London hospitals for treatment – Bart's, Guy's and St Thomas's all refused to

139. Dr William Marsden

take her in because she did not have a letter of introduction from a hospital sponsor. The girl died within two days and Marsden determined to amend the situation so that free treatment was available for those who were outside the conventional system. That was the genesis of the Royal Free Hospital, which was founded in the Hatton Garden area.

Marsden's interest in the treatment of cancer may have been caused by his own wife's death from the disease. He believed that a specialist hospital for its treatment was needed, though he met opposition from Queen Victoria who saw no need for hospitals devoted to a single illness, and from the *British Medical Journal*, which in 1860 proclaimed 'We are afraid the public are not yet in any way indoctrinated with the present professional feelings against the evils of special hospitals. One of the most unjustifiable of these institutions is the Cancer Hospital founded by Dr William Marsden and now rebuilding in the Brompton [sic] Road.'

Marsden's hospital was the first in the world specifically to treat cancer. It began as an outpatients' dispensary in Cannon Row, Westminster in 1851, and then moved on to a house on the corner of Hollywood Road and Fulham Road with 26 beds. In 1862 his new hospital was built on the Chelsea side of Fulham Road on an acre of land that cost £4500. The building, which is now the centre block of the present enlarged hospital, had 70 beds. The foundation stone was laid in 1859 by the heiress, Angela Burdett-Coutts, who was a strong supporter of the enterprise. The two turreted wings were added in 1883.

The name of the hospital is a comparatively recent one, having been used only since 1954. It was called the Cancer Hospital for much of its life and became the Royal Cancer Hospital in 1936 when Edward VIII was patron.

The Royal Military Asylum

Passing the development of apartments and retail outlets called Duke of York Square now proceeding at the former Duke of Yorks Territorial Army Headquarters at the eastern end of the King's Road, you are also adjacent to a much older institution, the Royal Military Asylum for the Children of Soldiers of the Regular Army. Its moving spirit in 1799 was Secretary of War, William Windham, who envisaged a boarding school for orphans of soldiers. He noted, rather depressingly, that as the proposed site was near to the Royal Hospital for pensioners, the pupils might receive asylum at both ends of their lives within the same area.

The Asylum's patron was the legendary Grand Old Duke of York, immortalised in a derisory song, but it was the state which funded the school's activities, an early example of government funding of education.

The buildings were constructed to take 700 boys and 300 girls and opened to the first 200 pupils in 1803. The Asylum was designed in plain classical style by John Sanders at a cost of nearly £105,000. The girls were moved out to a new school in Southampton between 1816 and 1827, 'to the apparent and subsequent peace of the authorities at Chelsea', according to the

140. The Royal Military Asylum, the Duke of York's School, 1801.

141. Lessons at the Royal Military Asylum. By Rowlandson and Pugin c.1810.

School Chronicle of 1899.

The pupils became a familiar sight in Chelsea, as they often put on displays in the grounds. In 1909 the boys were moved to new buildings in Dover where the school still survives, and their old building then became the London headquarters of the Territorial Army.

The buildings and their capacious grounds were, of course, a commercially tantalising possession, and it was no surprise, when the Territorial Army left, that rumours of development, even demolition, circulated. The present scheme, which is the result of long-running discussions between the developers, the borough council and the Chelsea Society opened in April 2003.

Royal Mistresses

At least two royal mistresses have lived in Chelsea, Dorothy Jordan and Lillie Langtry. Mrs Jordan (1762-1816), a name she adopted, arrived penniless (and pregnant) from Ireland with her mother in 1782. She had already appeared on stage in Ireland, and eventually was engaged to appear at Drury Lane Theatre. By one critic she was pronounced 'a mere piece of theatrical mediocrity', while Byron thought her superb. She caught the eye, as they say, of the unmarried Duke of Clarence (the future William IV) in 1790, and by him had ten children. She already had a daughter by her theatre manager in Dublin, and in London a further four by Sir Richard Ford.

Her relationship with Clarence was a good one, until George III, concerned that none of his sons had produced a legitimate heir, ordered them to marry and produce one. Clarence abandoned Mrs Jordan and did as he was told and produced several children, none of whom survived infancy.

Jordan's Chelsea days were late in her life. In 1812 she was at 30 Cadogan Place.

Lillie Langtry (1853-1929) was an actress *after* she became the mistress of the Prince of Wales, the future Edward VII. Before that she was a decorous socialite, married to a shipowner, but her liaison with the future king helped her on to a stage career once he had severed the relationship. At various

142. Dorothy Jordan.

143. Lillie Langtry.

144. Bertrand Russell.

times she was at 37 Ovington Square, 18 Pont Street and 15 Tedworth Square, a house which she later sold to the famous cricketer 'Plum' Warner.

Bertrand Russell

The philosopher Bertrand Russell (1872-1970) had a number of Chelsea addresses. The first was at 14 Cheyne Walk, where he rented rooms in the autumn of 1902. He was then aged 30, and engaged in completing one of his major works *The Principles of Mathematics*. He was also consumed by personal problems. Though already married himself, he was in love with Evelyn, the wife of his close associate Alfred Whitehead, who with Russell wrote *Principia Mathematica*.

Russell returned to this road in 1903 when he was at no. 13, and a year later was back at no. 14. In the spring of 1905 he rented 4 Ralston Street. Russell subsequently fell in love with Lady Ottoline Morrell, and occasionally met her at Whitehead's house at 17 Carlyle Square. Whitehead later moved to 12 Elm Park Gardens, while

Russell languished in Brixton gaol for opposing Britain's participation in the 1st World War.

Russell married his second wife, Dora, at Chelsea Registry Office in 1921, six days after his divorce from his first wife, Alys, and by early November that year they were living at 31 Sydney Street. When Russell stood for the Labour Party as parliamentary candidate, George Bernard Shaw commented that in Chelsea, 'no Progressive has a dog's chance'.

Russell spent much of his later years in north Wales with his fourth wife, though with a pied à terre at 43 Hasker Street

St Luke

Long before Chelsea's focus moved northwards to the King's Road, a new parish church was built, north of that thoroughfare. The Old Church by the riverside was small and congested, and as early as 1751 the Vestry considered whether to enlarge it, rebuild it or build a new church elsewhere. Inevitably, the cheapest option was adopted and they made do with the old building, fearing the expense of a new building. But by 1806 the Vestry

was prepared to be more realistic. The resolution it passed that year demonstrates that already the population of Chelsea in its northern parts was significant, despite the fact that the eastern end of King's Road (*qv*) was then, in theory, a closed royal highway. The Vestry proposed that 'considering the bad state of the present church, it not being large enough to the accommodation of this populous parish, and above all its distance from the most populous parts, that it be recommended, instead of repairing it, that measures be resorted to for erecting a new one in a more central spot.'

The resolution that time was lost, but in 1815 the Archdeacon pressed for repairs of the Old Church and for more accommodation for the populace. This led, in 1818, to a decision to erect a new building. The burial ground in Sydney Street seemed the appropriate site.

Building began in 1820 and the church was consecrated in 1824, though the projected spire was never built. The Duke of Wellington had been due to lay the foundation stone, but because of indisposition, his brother, Dr Wellesley, the rector of Chelsea, did the honours.

The church, an early exercise

145. *A south-west view of St Luke's church, from an original drawing by the architect, 1822.*

in Gothic revival, was designed by James Savage.

Charles Dickens was married here in 1836 to Catherine Hogarth, whose parents lived in the Fulham Road.

St Mark's College

Before the passing of the 1870 Education Act almost all education, outside the charity schools, was governed by the Church, usually via the agency of the National Society for the Education of the Poor in the Principles of the Established Church. There were also schools for nonconformist families run by the British and Foreign School Society. Therefore, when in 1835 Parliament voted money to be spent on training teachers, the question was, should it be spent on Church of England schools only? The matter was still unresolved when the National Society bought a large house to the very west of Chelsea, standing on the upper part of the Creek between Fulham and King's Roads, called Stanley House, to be a college for their own schoolmasters.

The first principal, when the college opened in 1841, was the Rev. Derwent Coleridge, son of the poet. Gladstone was a keen supporter.

The Society added a children's school to the original building, an octagonal structure shown in illustration 146, so that the trainee teachers had pupils on which to practise.

The school was later merged with another and moved to Plymouth. Of recent years the buildings have been used by King's College.

Stanley House was not the

147. An examination of students at the Coilege in the 1870s, as depicted in the Illustrated London News.

146. The school, including the octagonal building, in the foreground, and St Mark's College to the rear.

first building on the site. An earlier house was built by Sir Arthur Gorges, a friend of the poet Edmund Spenser. Gorges, a cousin of Sir Walter Raleigh, and like him a naval man, died in 1625 and in 1637 the property passed into the possession of his daughter, the wife of Sir Robert Stanley. The house was rebuilt towards the end of the seventeenth century.

John Sandoe

The oldest established bookshop in Chelsea is that of John Sandoe at 10 Blacklands Terrace. According to an article by Johnny de Falbe in the *Chelsea Society Annual Report* (1999), when Mr Sandoe took the then unpromising premises in 1957 they had previously been used by three separate concerns at the same time – a dress shop (before that it had been a poodle parlour), a secondhand bookshop and a secretarial business.

149. Self-portrait of John Singer Sargent.

John Singer Sargent

The American, John Singer Sargent (1856-1925), actually born in Florence, became one of the most important portrait painters of his time. He began his artistic career with very little money indeed. When asked to do a portrait of Robert Louis Stevenson he had to borrow the train fare down to the writer's home in Bournemouth. In his prime, and before he decided to stop doing portraits, many famous people came to sit for him in his studio in Tite Street, where he also had his residence next door at no. 11. One of his sitters was the actress, Ellen Terry *(qv)*. He remained unmarried and relied for family life at his sister's flat in Carlyle Mansions. By the 1890s his fee for a portrait was 1000 guineas, a fabulous sum. At his parties in Tite Street he introduced the music of his friend Gabriel Fauré and, later, that of Percy Grainger.

He died after spending an evening with his sister and reading some Voltaire.

Shops and traders

As shown in the page from Kelly's Directory of 1906, shown in illustration 88, the shops and indeed the trades of King's Road were of an entirely different

148. The Royal Cadogan Dairy in Chelsea.

150. *Goss's Pharmacy in Sloane Street, on the verge of demolition, early in the 20th century.*

subsequently called. Shrewsbury House was demolished in 1813, although parts remained in houses in Cheyne Walk in 1928.

Silkworms in Chelsea

Just as the Chelsea Porcelain Factory *(qv)* sought to create china as good as any imported from the Orient, so a serious attempt was made to make silk in Chelsea for the same reason.

Silk thread was produced by silkworms which thrived on mulberry trees. At least two attempts in London had been made to grow mulberry trees so as to foster the breeding of silkworms on a commercial scale. One was as early as 1548 in the grounds of Syon House and, more seriously, King James I attempted to set up an enterprise in the grounds of today's Buckingham Palace. Both ventures failed, but a new attempt was made in Chelsea in the 18th century.

The experiment took place on some land called Sandhills, part of Sir Thomas More's old estate, bounded by Fulham Road and King's Road, and by Park Walk and Old Church Street. The idea was that of Henry Barham, a surgeon who had practised in Jamaica, and had settled in Chelsea *c*.1716. He persuaded, one, John Appletree to take out a patent in 1718 for the production of raw silk and to issue shares for its exploitation. The total number of shares was to be 10,000, valued at £5 each: it was estimated that the actual laying out of the gardens and the planting of the trees would cost £25,000. Though attended by some initial success, the venture, just like its predecessors, closed after a few years. There are still mulberry trees in the area – Mulberry Walk commemorates this brief venture.

nature than today's. One of the most common businesses was the dairy, most of which had their own delivery service.

We show here *(ills 149-151)* three of the businesses of the late 19th and early 20th centuries.

Shrewsbury House

This house was built by 1519, situated by the river between today's Cheyne Row and Oakley Street. The 4th Earl of Shrewsbury, the occupier, was Privy Councillor to Henry VIII, and his son Richard was born at Chelsea. The 6th Earl, who was the fourth (and most unhappy) husband of the famous 'Bess of Hardwick', left the house to her. With other properties, including Hardwick Hall, she was the wealthiest woman in England excepting the Queen. Though she had four houses in which she could stay when called to London by her husband's death in 1590, she chose Chelsea and arrived with a considerable retinue.

The house was purchased in the 1640s by Sir Joseph Alston, after whom the house was often

151. Terrey's shop in Cheyne Walk, the site of Shrewsbury House. From a drawing by Hanslip Fletcher.

152. Shrewsbury House.

The Sitwells

The Sitwells are not to everyone's taste – too precious for many, and in the same league, in that respect as some of the Bloomsbury set. The Sitwells were at Swan Walk 1917-19, and then at 2 Carlyle Square, which Osbert Sitwell (1892-1969) was to occupy for 40 years. It was at this latter address that the young composer, William Walton, and the poet, Edith Sitwell (1887-1964), produced the first (private) performance of *Façade*. Edith was clothed in her usual medieval garb, intoning the words of her poetry from behind a curtain, to Walton's music.

Sir Hans Sloane

Apart from the Cadogans, no other person has left his name so indelibly in the Chelsea nomenclature. Apart from the

154. *Sir Hans Sloane, from a painting by Stephen Slaughter.*

obvious Sloane Square/Street and Hans Place, other street names derive indirectly from him, such as Paultons Square, Rysbrack Street, Tedworth Square – *see Street Name Derivations.*

Sloane (1660-1753) shone brightly in the world of medicine early in his life. He was elected a Fellow of the Royal Society at 25 (he was its president, following Newton, in 1727), and was elected to the Royal College of Physicians in 1687. In that year he went to the West Indies for 15 months and brought back with him 800 species of plants, many of which he donated to the Physic Garden at Chelsea (*qv*). He developed a great affection for the Garden and, when he bought the manor of Chelsea in 1712, he ensured that the Society of Apothecaries had a freehold of the site as long as the Garden produced new species each year.

In his house at Bloomsbury, which was also his practice address, he amassed a vast library of 50,000 books and over 3,000 volumes of manuscripts, 347 volumes of drawings and illuminated books, 32,000 coins and many natural specimens. He

153. *Properties in Sloane Square, 1892, about to be demolished.*

moved all these on his retirement to Chelsea in 1742, where he lived in the manor house built for Henry VIII. Sloane had directed that on his death (which occurred in 1753, when he was 92) his entire collection should be offered to the country at a nominal price and kept together at Chelsea. This was not to be. A grudging, cheeseparing government was finally persuaded to buy the collection at the price specified, but it was housed instead at Montagu House in Bloomsbury, where it became one of the keystones of the British Museum – an appropriate address, as it happens, since in his early days as a physician Sloane himself had lodged there before he moved on to Bloomsbury Place.

Upon his death the Chelsea manor was divided between his two daughters, one of whom had married into the Cadogan family.

Sloane Square

In 1771 Sloane Square was enclosed and cobbled, but Horwood's map of the early 19th century shows it crisscrossed by roads – one leading from Sloane Street into Lower Sloane Street, and the other, at a diagonal, continuing the King's Road route from west to east, into today's Cliveden Place. Buildings surrounded it, including a stone yard on the site of Peter Jones. The roads were still there at the end of the century, although by then the tracks of the District Line had been laid beneath it, on their way to South Kensington. In 1927 an experimental one-way traffic system was introduced, made permanent in 1929.

The large brick and stone building on the south side of the Square was designed by Amos Faulkner and developed by William Willett, the inventor of 'daylight saving' in 1906.

Sloane Square Station

Chelsea's only underground station opened on Christmas Eve 1868 as part of the District Line's route to South Kensington. Over three thousand men were employed in the haste to have that section of the line (then just from South Kensington to Westminster) open for Christmas traffic. The railway was constructed throughout by the cut-and-cover method – that is, it was excavated from the surface, the sides lined, the track laid, and then a roof put on. Unfortunately for Chelsea, it was not possible by this technique to continue the line along the King's Road, even if the proprietors had wished to, because of the nature of the land here.

A well-known feature of the station is that the river Westbourne (qv), now the Ranelagh Sewer, crosses the tracks in a diagonally placed casing (see ill. 156).

155. Sloane Square, c.1904.

156. *Sloane Square station in the 1920s, with the river Westbourne diverted across its tracks.*

Slums

The Chelsea of today seems a far cry from slum property, but it is interesting to note that Dickens in *Nicholas Nickleby* wrote that 'Cadogan Place was the connecting link between the aristocratic pavements of Belgravia and the barbarism of Chelsea'. Dickens, of course, was prone to exaggeration, but it is worth also noting that Chelsea's Medical Officer in 1900 claimed that 'We have much improved our own sewers and house drains, roads have also been widened, open spaces secured for the public and some of the worst slums of old Chelsea have been demolished.' Note the word 'some'.

The Cadogan estate bulldozed a great deal of Chelsea between Cadogan Square and the King's Road in their early 20th-century rebuilding. The *Daily Chronicle* in 1909 complained of '20,000 people being driven from Chelsea so that the members of one particular family should be enriched.' The area housed many of those who serviced and supplied the rich of Hans Town – chimney sweeps, traders, coal men and the like. Probably because of the outbreak of the 1st World War the Cadogan development plans took a long time to proceed, because by the 1930s many of the old residents were still in place, and militant enough to face the bulldozers. An Eviction Defence Army of about 300 fought off demolition workers with noise, sticks and whistles, but to no avail.

This was not the only area of slum property in Chelsea – that around Lots Road lasted until modern times. Judging from Hedderley's photograph of 1892 *(ill. 153)* Sloane Square itself was very run down and unworthy, architecturally, to be Chelsea's introductory thoroughfare. The properties, shown in the photograph as derelict, were demolished soon afterwards.

Philip Wilson Steer

The painter Philip Wilson Steer (1860-1942) lived for at least 45 years in Chelsea, from 1898-1942 at 109 Cheyne Walk, where he was surrounded by bric-a-brac and cats. Previously he had had studios in Manresa Road and Sydney Mews. His residence in Chelsea coincided with that of Augustus John and there the similarity ended. Steer was an inarticulate man, reserved and self-effacing. He did not, as John did, dress up as an artist. Instead Steer wore, even when teaching at the Slade, a formal suit, winged collar and a bow tie. He was prominent in the important New English Art Club movement of the later part of the 19th century, and was also a founder-member of the Chelsea Arts Club (*qv*).

Street Name Derivations

Alexander Square SW3. From the owner of the Thurloe estate, John Alexander (1762-1831).

Anderson Street SW3. John Anderson was a trustee of James Colvill, whose nursery ground was on the site.

Ann Lane SW10. Probably after the wife of the builder of nearby Riley Street *(qv)*.

Apollo Place SW10. Built on Riley's land *(see Riley Street)* and probably named after a local public house.

Ashburnham Road SW10. From Ashburnham House, home of the Earls of Ashburnham, which stood here until *c.*1880.

Beaufort Street. From Beaufort House, once owned by Sir Thomas More *(qv)* and later by Henry, Duke of Beaufort. The house, situated at the lower end of the street, was demolished by Sir Hans Sloane after 1737, when the street was formed.

Blacklands Terrace, SW3. In a survey of Chelsea in 1544 this area was known as 'Blacklande'.

Bramerton Street SW3. Derivation unknown, but it is a Norfolk place name.

Bray Place SW3. A significant grant of manorial property and land was made to Sir Reginald Bray (d.1503) by Henry VII in recognition of Bray's help in the king's bid to gain the crown.

Britten Street SW3. J Britten was a trustee of the nearby church of St Luke, built about the same time as the street.

Burnsall Street SW3. The road was called Brewer Street up to 1928, when it was renamed in memory of Martha Burnsall, who had established a charity for 'poor decayed housekeepers' in 1805.

Bury Walk SW3. Possibly because it led to a burial ground, the site of which was later taken by St Luke's church.

Bywater Street SW3. Thomas Bywater was a landowner in the area.

Cale Street SW3. Judith Cale (d.1717) established an annual fund of 23 shillings each for six poor widows.

Callow Street SW3. John Callow, from a family of Chelsea publicans, established a building business *c.*1840 and was employed by the Cadogans in laying out a number of Chelsea streets.

Camera Place SW3. Origin unknown. Nearby was Camera Square, now superseded by Chelsea Park Gardens.

Carlyle Square SW3. Once called Oakley Square, it was renamed in 1872 in honour of Thomas Carlyle *(qv)*, long-time resident of Cheyne Row.

Caversham Street SW3. A subsidiary title of the Earls Cadogan.

Chelsea Park Gardens SW3. On part of the land owned and imparked by Sir Thomas More in the time of Henry VIII. It superseded Camera Square.

Cheltenham Terrace SW3. John Tombs, its builder in the 1840s, came from Upton St Leonard's, near Cheltenham.

Cheyne Row and Cheyne Walk SW3. The Cheynes were Lords of Chelsea Manor.

Christchurch Street SW3. After Christchurch in Flood Street.

Coulson Street SW3. Thomas Coulson, a Clerkenwell butcher, was heir to James Colvill, nursery ground owner in the first half of the 19th century. *(See also Anderson Street)*.

Cremorne Road SW10. After Cremorne Gardens *(qv)*.

Culford Gardens SW3. Culford Hall, near Bury St Edmunds, was a Cadogan family property.

Danube Street SW3. Formerly called Little Blenheim Street (named after Marlborough's victory) – the village of Blenheim stands on the river Danube.

Danvers Street SW3. Sir John Danvers' house *(qv)* stood on the site of Danvers Street and Paultons Square.

Denyer Street SW3. Elizabeth Denyer left an annual fund to be distributed among eight poor spinsters in Chelsea.

Dilke Street SW3. It is most likely that this street was named after the radical MP for Chelsea 1868-86, Sir Charles Dilke, who was born and lived for many years in Sloane Street, rather than, as has been suggested elsewhere, his antiquarian father of the same name. The street was named in 1875 when Dilke *(qv)* was MP, but his political career was terminated when he was cited as a co-respondent in a divorce case – a charge he strenuously denied.

Donne Place SW3. John Donne (1573-1631), the poet, stayed for a period at Danvers House.

Dovehouse Street SW3. A dovecote is shown here in Dovehouse Close on Hamilton's 1664 map of Chelsea.

Draycott Avenue, Terrace and Place SW3. Nearby stood Blacklands House, once leased by Sir Francis Shuckburgh, who was married to Anna Maria Draycott.

Durham Place SW3. Nearby stood Durham House, a 16th-century mansion demolished *c.*1920.

Elm Park Gardens/Lane/Road SW10. A prominent elm tree stood in this vicinity under which, so legend has it, Queen Elizabeth sheltered during a rain storm. The 'Queenes tree' is mentioned in contemporary parish records, so that the legend, for once, may have some veracity.

Elystan Street SW3. An ancestral family name of the Cadogans.

Flood Street SW3. Luke Thomas Flood, who lived in Cheyne Row, left £3000 to the parish in 1860 for charitable uses.

Franklin's Row SW3. The Franklin family owned a field in this neighbourhood in the 18th century.

Glebe Place SW3. Built on the glebe lands belonging to Chelsea Rectory.

157. Glebe Place, c.1905.

Godfrey Street SW3. Origin uncertain. Possibly named from Walter Godfrey a Chelsea land-owner, or corn chandler John Godfrey, who held land by the King's Road in the 1830s.

Guthrie Street SW3. George James Guthrie (1785-1856), an army surgeon, popularised new treatments for amputations and gunshot wounds during the Napoleonic wars.

Hemus Place SW3. William Hemus Rayner was a Cadogan family builder, but the road was not named after him until 1937.

Henniker Mews SW3. John Wright Henniker Wilson married Mary, the heiress of Chelsea Park.

Ixworth Place SW3. The Cadogan family owned Culford near Ixworth, in Suffolk.

Jubilee Place SW3. So named in 1810 to celebrate the 50th anniversary of George III's reign.

King's Road SW3, SW10. The section of this main highway, from Sloane Square to Old Church Street, was once a pri-vate royal road. It was desig-nated a public road in 1830.

Langton Street SW3. Thomas Langton, a Lambeth timber mer-chant, built in this area in the 1850s.

Lawrence Street SW3. Thomas Lawrence bought the former Chelsea Manor House *(qv)* in the 1580s. A number of family monuments may be seen in Chelsea Old Church. The house was demolished early in the 18th century and the street gradually formed.

Limerston Street SW3. Named after a village in the Isle of Wight.

Lincoln Street SW3. Stroud Lincoln was another executor of the will of James Colvill, owner of a nearby nursery ground. *(See Anderson Street.)*

Mallord Street SW3. Named in 1909 after the painter Joseph Mallord William Turner (1775-1851), who lived at 119 Cheyne Walk in his later years.

Margaretta Terrace SW3. Margaretta was the wife of the eccentric Dr Phené *(qv)*, who de-veloped this terrace.

Markham Square/Street SW3. The Markham Evans family owned Box Farm in this vicinity from c.1580. It was demolished c.1900.

Marlborough Street SW3. The 3rd Duke of Marlborough (1706-58) lived in a house by Chelsea Common towards the end of his life.

Milman's Street SW10. Sir William Milman, having made a fortune trading stocks, built some streets in Holborn – Millman Street there is named after him. He bought a house in Chelsea in 1697 and was buried in Chelsea Old Church in 1713.

Milner Street SW3. Richard Moore owned land hereabouts which he divided between his five children, one of whom, Mary Jane, married Colonel Charles Milner.

Moore Street SW3. See Milner Street above.

Moravian Place SW10. The Moravian protestant commu-

158. *St Loo Avenue and Rossetti Mansions c.1905.*

nity *(qv)* was established in Chelsea in the 1750s. Its burial ground adjoins this road.

Mossop Street SW3. Named in 1935, it commemorates either or both Henry Mossop, an 18th-century actor who lost most of his money gambling, or Charles Mossop, active in local politics in the 19th century. The former was buried in Chelsea Old Church.

Mulberry Walk SW3. An attempt was made to begin a silk producing farm at Chelsea Park in 1719. Large numbers of silkworms *(qv)* were imported once mulberry trees, which they feed on, were grown. The worms did not take to the English climate, but it is thought that at least one of the trees survives.

Oakley Street SW3. William Cadogan was created Baron Cadogan of Oakley in 1718.

Ormonde Gate SW3. Indicates the proximity of old Ormonde House *(qv)*.

Park Walk SW10. Built on the western part of Chelsea Park.

Paultons Square SW3. The eldest daughter of Sir Hans Sloane married George Stanley of Paultons, Hampshire. The square stands on their land.

Petyt Place. Named in 1895 after lawyer and antiquarian William Petyt (1636-1707), who occupied a house nearby.

Petyward SW3. The Pettiward family owned land in the vicinity in the 17th century.

Phené Street SW3. The eccentric Dr John Samuel Phené *(qv)* was responsible for developments in this area.

Pond Place SW3. This road marks the footpath at the edge of Chelsea Common, where a large pond existed. Flats now stand on the pond's site.

Queen's Elm Square SW3. See Elm Park Gardens.

Radnor Walk SW3. After the death of the Earl of Radnor in 1685 his widow, Letitia, married Charles, Lord Cheyne, lord of Chelsea Manor. They lived at Radnor House in this vicin-

ity until Cheyne's death in 1698. The house was demolished in 1888. The street was named in 1937.

Rawlings Street SW3. Named in memory of Charles Rawlings who left £400 for the parish poor when he died in 1862.

Red Anchor Close SW3. Indicates the nearby location of the Chelsea Porcelain factory in Lawrence Street, which had a red anchor as one of its maker's marks.

Riley Street SW10. Land here was leased by Stephen Riley, an upholsterer, who later married its owner, Mary Ann Jones.

Rosemoor Street SW3. A Cadogan residence in Torrington, Devon.

Rysbrack Street SW3. John Michael Rysbrack (1693-1770) was the sculptor of the statue of Sir Hans Sloane which stands in the Chelsea Physic Garden.

St Leonard's Terrace SW3. Its builder, John Tombs, came from Upton St Leonards near Cheltenham. *See also* Cheltenham Terrace.

St Loo Avenue SW3. The re-

159. Sydney Street, c.1904.

Sprimont Place SW3. Named in 1937 to commemorate Nicholas Sprimont, manager of the Chelsea Porcelain factory *(qv)* from 1745-1769.

Stackhouse Street SW3. Named in 1938 to commemorate the Rev. Thomas Stackhouse (1677-1752), a Chelsea resident.

Stewart's Grove SW3. Land here was leased of the Cadogan family by William Stewart, auctioneer of Piccadilly, in 1810. He began to build on it in 1827.

Swan Walk SW3. The Old Swan Inn *(qv)* by the Physic Garden, was a popular London resort, visited a number of times by Pepys. It was also the finishing post for Doggett's Coat and Badge race on the river *(qv)*.

Sydney Street SW3. Built in 1845 across the land of the Smith Charity Estate, a trustee of which was John Robert, Viscount Sydney.

Tadema Road SW10. Named in 1878, probably after the

doubtable Lady St Loo, better known as Bess of Hardwick (1518-1608), was Countess of Shrewsbury, whose husband owned Shrewsbury House in Cheyne Walk.

Shalcomb Street SW3. Named after a village in the Isle of Wight.

Sloane Avenue/Square/Street SW3. Sir Hans Sloane (1660-1753) *(qv)* was Chelsea's lord of the manor in 1712, and lived in Chelsea from 1741 until his death.

Smith Street SW3. The builder of the street *c.*1800 was Thomas Smith, a former vintner.

160. Tite Street, c.1904.

161. Walpole Street, c.1850.

Dutch artist, Sir Lawrence Alma-Tadema, who settled in England in 1870.

Tedworth Square SW3. A Sloane family name – the wife of the Rev. George Sloane-Stanley came from Tedworth in Hampshire.

Tite Street SW3. A street built soon after the death of Sir William Tite MP (1798-1873) who had been closely concerned with the construction of the Thames Embankment.

Tryon Street SW3. Named in 1913 to commemorate Vice Admiral Sir George Tryon, drowned in 1893 after a collision during Fleet manoeuvres. The street was previously part of Keppel Street.

The Vale SW3. Built partly on a paddock belonging to Vale Grove, a villa in Old Church Street.

Walpole Street SW3. Sir Robert Walpole lived in the vicinity before moving to a house which became the Royal Hospital Infirmary.

Walton Street SW3. From George Walton Onslow, a trustee of the Smith Charity based in Kensington.

Wellington Square SW3. Built c.1852 and named to commemorate the first Duke of Wellington, whose body lay in state at the Royal Hospital Chelsea in 1852 before his funeral at St Paul's Cathedral. His brother was Rector of Chelsea 1805-36.

Whitehead's Grove SW3. William Whitehead leased Chelsea Common in 1810 from the Cadogan family and promptly built this street.

Woodfall Street SW3. Henry Sampson Woodfall (1739-1805) was a famous printer of his time, and also a resident of Cheyne Walk.

The Swan

The Old Swan stood east of the Physic Garden, right on the riverside, with steps down to the water. How old it was is uncertain, but it was there in 1666 and an established place for Londoners to come by road, or more likely by river, for a day out. However, when Pepys wanted to visit it that year, he left in a hurry. On 9 April 1666 Pepys records:

'By coach to Mrs Pierce's and with her and Knopp and Mrs Pierce's boy and girl abroad, thinking to have been merry at Chelsea; but being come almost to the house by coach near the waterside, a house alone, I think the Swan, a gentleman walking by called to us to tell us that the house was shut up of the sickness [the Plague]. So we with great affright turned back, being

115

162. *The Old Swan at Chelsea riverside. From a painting by G Lambert, c.1857.*

163. *Playing 'Three Corners' at the Swan in 1788.*

at the opening of the Theatre Royal Bath, wearing a dress designed for her by her future lover, architect Edward William Godwin – Godwin built Whistler's house in Tite Street, Chelsea. The following year she married the celebrated painter, George Frederick Watts. He had been entranced by her beauty but he could not cope with her youthfulness and a forced separation was made the following year. She then went to live with Godwin, had two children by him (which, curiously, are not mentioned in Godwin's entry in the *Dictionary of National Biography* – but then neither is Ellen Terry), Edith and Gordon Craig.

In 1876 she was at the Royal Court in Chelsea for a long run. Her career was an extended one and she was consistently popular and admired as an actress.

From 1904-1920 she lived at 215 King's Road – a house which still survives.

164. *Ellen Terry.*

holden to the gentlemen; and went away (I for my part in great disorder) for Kensington.'

The Old Swan, which was the finishing post for the annual Doggett Coat and Badge Race (*qv*) became also a brewery in 1780. It was demolished with the construction of the Embankment in the 1870s.

Ellen Terry

The actress Ellen Terry (1847-1928) was one of the beauties of her time. She was born into a theatrical family – both her parents, three of her sisters and a brother all went on the stage. Ellen first appeared in London as a boy in *A Winter's Tale* in 1856. In 1863 she played Tatiana

165. *A river party opposite Paradise Row, depicted by Rowlandson in 1807.*

The Thames

The derivation of the place-name Chelsea stems from the Thames, though the experts are divided on the precise root. Across the water, in the name Battersea, the 'ea' suffix means island, but with Chelsea an early form of the name, *Caelichyth*, suggests a landing place for chalk or limestone. Otherwise it has been suggested that another early form, *Chesil*, meaning gravel bank, as the derivation.

Because of the inadequacy of the roads, Chelsea necessarily centred on the river, within easy reach of Westminster and the more affluent of London's citizens who chose Chelsea for a country home. River views of Chelsea are thus relatively abundant.

For centuries the Thames and Chelsea were intimately associated and the river was the scene of many local trades and events. Barbara Denny described the re-

166. *Paradise Row from the Thames. From an engraving by Vivarez after Maurer.*

lationship between Chelsea and the Thames in her book *Chelsea Past*, 'This water bore Thomas More on his last voyage, heard the first playing of Handel's *Water Music*, carried kings and queens on great and fearful occasions, and inspired artists such as Turner and Whistler.'

But Chelsea's intimacy with the Thames was broken when the Embankment was constructed in the 1870s. This was not popular with those who enjoyed the aesthetic quiet of the riverside here, but without it Chelsea would have been inundated many times since.

167. The Old Church by the river, 1829.

168. Boats moored at Chelsea by Cadogan Pier in 1860.

169. Dame Sybil Thorndike and Sir Lewis Casson outside Chelsea Town Hall on polling day, 1964.

Thorndike and Casson

The grand theatrical couple, Sybil Thorndike (1882-1976) and Lewis Casson (1875-1969) lived in Chelsea most of their lives, at no. 6 Carlyle Square from 1921 to 1932, and then in a flat at 98 Swan Court, Manor Place.

Sybil Thorndike had initially wanted a musical career, but she developed a painful problem with her hands while playing the piano so that she could not span an octave.

She began her theatrical career during 1904-7 with a tour of America, where she played in numerous parts and productions. She met Casson in 1907, married him a year later, and became a close associate of George Bernard Shaw, who wrote *St Joan* for her to play the title role.

The couple celebrated their sixtieth wedding anniversary in 1968, and he died a year later.

170. J M W Turner, by E Wildman jnr.

171. Turner's house at 119 Cheyne Walk.

172. Entrance to the Victoria Hospital for Children.

J M W Turner

The painter, Joseph Mallord William Turner (1775-1851) in his later and most famous days became reclusive. By 1838 he had rented 119 Cheyne Walk under an assumed name, and was obsessive in retaining his anonymity amongst his neighbours in Chelsea. Here he assumed the name of 'Admiral' Booth, from Sarah Booth, his landlady at Margate where he often stayed, and who looked after him in Chelsea. He concealed his Chelsea life even from his household in central London.

Much of Turner's best work, in its most abstract form, was done at Chelsea where the river scene gave him inspiration. Leopold Martin, son of the artist John Martin, found on visiting Turner at Chelsea, that 'the house had but three windows in front and was miserable in every respect, furnished in poor fashion.' An old woman, (presumably Mrs Booth), served them bread and cheese with porter, but Turner seemed pleased with his life there. He pointed out the view from his single window saying, 'Here, you see my study; sky and water. Are they

not glorious? Here I have my lesson, night and day!'. The house survives.

So well did he conceal the whereabouts of his Chelsea refuge that it was only when his 'official' London housekeeper, Hannah Danby, found a letter in his coat pocket which gave some clue to its location, that he was traced there the day before he died in 1851.

By his complicated and contested will he left much of his unsold work to the National Gallery, most of which is now displayed in a special gallery at Tate Britain.

Mark Twain

It is appropriate that Twain (1835-1910) follows Turner in this alphabetically arranged book, for Twain described a painting by the great master as a 'tortoiseshell cat floundering in a plate of tomatoes'. Twain's residence at 23 Tedworth Square from October 1896 to the summer of 1898 was clouded by the death of his daughter Susy. Writing furiously to blot out the sadness this had caused him, he also had to pay off debts for the collapse of his investment in a

typesetting machine. Twain, incidentally, is thought to be the first author to have sent a *typed* manuscript to a publisher.

Victoria Hospital for Children

The Hospital was begun in Gough House in 1866 by a group of Chelsea residents. It aimed to provide for children who 'being afflicted by the providence of God are too often surrounded by wretched and unhealthy influence'. By 1890 the out-patient department was treating 1,500 children a week and a new building was erected adjoining. The hospital moved out in the 1960s to St George's Hospital, Tooting.

The Volunteers

In common with most other small towns in the hinterland of London, a volunteer fighting force was raised in Chelsea at the end of the 18th century to face possible invasion by Napoleon. Their colours (embroidered by Chelsea ladies) were presented at the Royal Hospital on 3 May 1799. By 1804 the force had been reformed as the Chel-

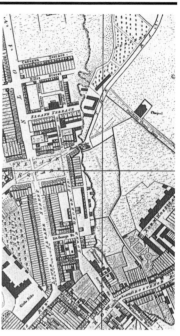

173. *The Victoria Hospital for Children in Cheyne Walk.*

174. *The Hans Town Volunteers in 1799.*

175. *The course of the river Westbourne at Chelsea's eastern boundary, in the early part of the 19th century.*

entirely underground as the Ranelagh Sewer. The outfall is sometimes visible at low tide and a Mr J D Carleton was once intrepid enough to walk up it from the Thames for several hundred yards.

Whistler in Chelsea

The painter, James Abbott McNeill Whistler (1834-1903), lived at an astonishing number of addresses in Chelsea. He was born in Massachusetts but from 1843 to 1849 he was in Russia where his father was the engineer for the new railway between St Petersburg and Moscow. 1855 found him in Paris, where he spent much time perfecting his etching techniques, and he was in London c.1859 staying at 62 Sloane Street with his half sister, Deborah and her husband. As from 1860 he settled in London and set about producing a

sea Association, which attended in splendour at a Jubilee celebration for George III at Cremorne Villa, at which their new colours had been embroidered by Queen Charlotte and daughters.

Such volunteer forces were not, in the event, needed and were disbanded.

The River Westbourne

The Westbourne forms the eastern boundary of Chelsea. Various tributaries rise in West Hampstead, join up at Kilburn, and the river flows down to Paddington, Bayswater Road and Hyde Park and then crosses beneath the road at Knightsbridge, very near to Harvey Nichols. It then meanders east of Cadogan Place to Sloane Square (where it now crosses above the tracks of the District Line) and out to the Thames west of Chelsea Bridge.

Some parts of it remained open until c.1856, but it is now

176. *Whistler in his studio, by Walter Greaves. The main painting is of Whistler's mother.*

series of etchings based on the Thames. His submissions to the Royal Academy in 1861 gave his address as 47 Hans Place, and the following two years at 12 Sloane Street. In 1863 he was at 101 Cheyne Walk.

By then he was strongly influenced by Japanese art and in this period he painted his famous picture of Old Battersea Bridge. His paintings were popular and many were exhibited at the Royal Academy, but, much to his irritation, the Academy did not make him a member.

From 1866 to 1878 he lived at 96 Cheyne Walk. This was a productive and remunerative

period for him, which included the commission to paint the Peacock Room for Frederick Leyland – now in America because of Leyland's dislike of the result. His work of this period also included the well-known portrait of Thomas Carlyle (*qv*).

Whistler then moved to the White House at 35 Tite Street, a house built for him by Edward William Godwin, whose widow he would later marry. His stay here was destined to be short, for on the basis of a painting he had exhibited at the Grosvenor Gallery, entitled *The Falling Rocket, Nocturne in Black and Gold*, he was accused by Ruskin of being a 'coxcomb' for asking

200 guineas for 'throwing a pot of paint in the public face'. Whistler sued for libel, won his case, but received only one farthing damages and was asked to pay his own considerable costs. He had to sell his beautiful house (which was, alas, demolished in 1965) and went bankrupt.

Whistler then went to Venice, was back in London in 1880, and in 1881 settled once more in Tite Street, this time at no. 13. He was at 2 The Vale in 1886, and then on to 454 Fulham Road. His last Chelsea address from *c*.1902 was 74 Cheyne Walk, built by C R Ashbee (*qv*), where he died. He is buried in Chiswick Old Cemetery.

177. *May Day celebrations at Whitelands College in 1904.*

Whitelands College

Whitelands College, a teacher training college now in Putney, originated in the King's Road. It was at Whitelands Lodge, a house to the west of the Royal Military Asylum, at the junction with Walpole Street. A girls' school existed here in the 18th century – Lord Nelson's niece was a pupil. In 1772 the Rev. Jenkins lectured here on 'Female Education and Christian Fortitude under Affliction'. The National Society instituted a training school for women teachers here in 1842. The old house was demolished in 1891 to be relaced by a new building by Henry Clutton. The school had an annual May Day festival overseen by John Ruskin *(ill. 177)*, and Burne-Jones designed stained glass windows for the chapel. With the lease expiring and the building by then too small, the College moved out in 1931 to West Hill, Putney and a block of flats, called Whitelands, was built on its site.

178. *Oscar Wilde; caricature by 'Ape' in Vanity Fair, 24 May 1884.*

Oscar Wilde

The career of Oscar Wilde (1854-1900), his descent from Society's favourite to an absurd prison sentence for homosexual behaviour, is well known and hardly bears retelling.

It was during his Chelsea days that the most dramatic events of his life occurred. Just like Whistler, Wilde was devoted to Tite Street, and first moved there in 1880. But he had earlier been in Oakley Street in 1876, when his mother took a house at no. 87 (it is now demolished). In 1881 Wilde was at 44 Tite Street, and then when he married Constance Lloyd in 1884, they moved into no. 34, a house transformed by Edward William Godwin who, as we have seen above, also built a house in the street for Whistler *(qv)*.

1891 saw the publication of *The Picture of Dorian Gray*. In 1892 *Lady Windermere's Fan*, his first comedy of manners, was staged and a year later came *A Woman of No Importance*; both of these were great successes. In 1893 his play *Salomé* was barred performance in England by the Lord Chamberlain's Office.

The year 1895, while he was still at no. 34 Tite Street, was his most turbulent. *The Ideal Husband* was produced in January, and his most famous play, *The Importance of Being Earnest*, a 'trivial comedy for serious people', was staged in February. At this time Wilde was famously insulted in a note from the Marquis of Queensberry, the father of his male lover, Lord Douglas, and in retaliation Wilde unwisely sued the Marquis for criminal libel. In the event Wilde lost his suit and was himself charged with homosexual behaviour.

It is indicative of the official moral outlook and inhibitions of the times, that when Wilde's grossly inadequate biography was written for the *Dictionary of National Biography*, the reason for Queensberry's remarks and the accusations made against Wilde at his trial are not described. Like Queen Victoria, who did not think that lesbianism existed, so the *DNB* did not wish to put a name to its male counterpart.

It is interesting to note that the judge at his trial, who gave him two years' hard labour, was a neighbour in Tite Street. After the trial verdict, Sir George Alexander, the actor-manager of St James's Theatre and also a neighbour at 57 Pont Street, who had made a great deal of money producing Wilde's plays, disloyally blanked out Wilde's name on the theatre's billboards which still carried on them the advertisements for Wilde's plays. To be fair, Alexander did bequeath the acting rights of the plays to Wilde's son Vyvyan Holland.

That was really the end of Wilde for Chelsea and indeed for London. He languished in Reading gaol, and on release fled to France where he died. He was buried in Paris.

Winchester House

This large house overlooking the river was built by James, Duke of Hamilton, c.1640 on some of the garden ground of Henry VIII's manor house. Sited to the east of today's Oakley Street it was bought in 1664 by the bishopric of Winchester as a London home for bishops of Winchester.

The house is described as 'a heavy brick building of low proportions and quite devoid of any architectural ornament, the interior fairly commodious and much enriched by collections of antiques'

The Chelsea historian Thomas Faulkner (*qv*) noted that 'the great staircase at the western end of the hall led to three grand drawing-rooms, which extended the whole length of the south front, and which, during the residence of the late bishop, were splendidly furnished.'

Winchester House was demolished in 1828 to be replaced by houses in Cheyne Walk and Oakley Street.

179. Winchester House in c.1810.

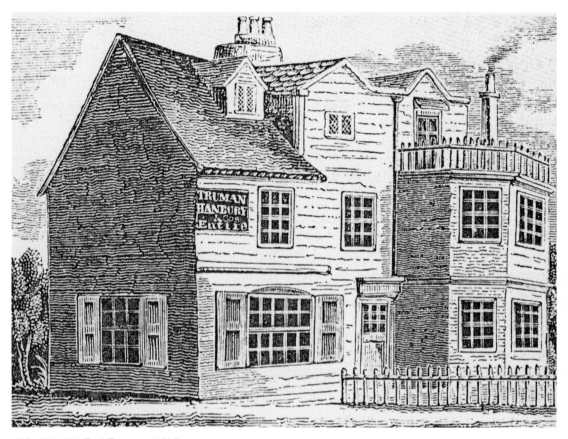

180. *World's End Tavern c.1828.*

181. *World's End Passage and old Battersea Bridge, by Walter Greaves.*

World's End

An inn existed here in the reign of Charles II and is mentioned in Congreve's *Love for Love* (1695). World's End was no doubt an ironic description of its isolation from areas of population, but it is not clear when it took on this lonely name. The pub itself was rebuilt very early in the twentieth century. The council housing estate in this area was designed by Eric Lyons, Cadbury-Brown, Metcalf and Cunningham in 1977.

Further Reading

Barton, Nicholas: *The Lost Rivers of London* (1962; new edn 1992).

Beaver, Alfred: *Memorials of Old Chelsea* (1892).

Bignell, John: *Chelsea Seen from 1860 to 1980* (1978).

Blunt, Reginald: *The Carlyles' Chelsea Home* (1895)

Blunt, Reginald: *Paradise Row* (1906).

Blunt, Reginald: *In Cheyne Walk and Thereabout* (1914).

Blunt, Reginald: *The Wonderful Village* (1919).

Blunt, Reginald: *By Chelsea Reach* (1921).

Blunt, Reginald: *The Lure of Old Chelsea* (1922).

Blunt, Reginald: *The Crown and Anchor*(1925).

Bryan, George: *Chelsea in the olden and present times* (1869).

Bryan, Michael: *Chelsea and the Thames* (1989).

Chelsea Society Annual Reports 1927 to date

Clark, Roger: *Chelsea Today* (1991).

Curle, Brian: *Leaflet on Shrewsbury House* (Chelsea Library).

Curle, Brian and Pratt, Mrs P K, *Kensington and Chelsea Street Names* (1980).

Davies, Randall: *Chelsea Old Church* (1904).

Dean, Captain C G T: *The Royal Hospital Chelsea* (1950).

Denny, Barbara: *Chelsea Past* (1996).

Drewitt, F Dawtrey: *The romance of the Apothecaries' Garden at Chelsea* (1924).

Durrant, D N: 'Shrewsbury House' in *History Today*, July 1974.

Edmunds, Richard: *Chelsea: from the Five Fields to the World's End* (1956).

Faulkner, Thomas: *Historical and Topographical Description of Chelsea* (1829).

Gaunt, William: *Kensington and Chelsea* (rev. edn 1975).

Holme, Thea: *Chelsea* (1972).

Longford, Elizabeth, with Ditchburn, Jonathan: *Images of Chelsea* (1980).

Macdonald, Nesta: *The Pheasantry* (1977).

Matthews, Leslie: *Chelsea Old Church* 1941-50

Pearman, Robert: *The Cadogan Estate* (1986).

Pocok, Tom: *Chelsea Reach* (1970).

Scott, Walter Sidney: *Little Chelsea: being a topographical account of the parish... of St Peter's, Cranley Gardens in the 18th and early 19th centuries.* (1940).

Silver, Harold and Teague, John: *Chelsea College – A History* (1978).

Survey of London volumes: *The Parish of Chelsea* (pt I, 1909); (pt II, 1913); (pt III, *The Old Church*, 1921); (pt IV, *The Royal Hospital, Chelsea* 1927)

Willson, E J: *West London Nursery Gardens* (1982).

Index

Asterisks denote illustration or caption